WISDOM ROAD

'This book is a precious gift. It is light and yet goes to core of our identity. Very readable and simple yet deeply profound. It deals with the serious issues of life with humour and judgement.'
Richard Izard, Leadership Coach

'Viv brings wisdom out of the attic and into the 21st century. Whether you are old, young, thriving or failing, this book with enrich you, anchor you and help you live well.'
Madi Simpson, Bible teacher, writer and everyday parent

'In Wisdom Road Viv's voice comes through – an authentic, imaginative and faith-filled voice offering practical wisdom for life as it really is.'
Jez Barnes, Vicar, St Stephen's Twickenham

D1334082

WISDOM ROAD

Making decisions in company with God

VIV THOMAS

formation
developing spectacular ordinary lives

First published in Great Britain in 2016

Formation Global
76 Rannoch Road
London W6 9SP

www.formation.org.uk

A catalogue record for this book is available from the British Library

ISBN 978-0-9926312-1-5

Typeset by Thirteen Creative

For Alice and Issy

And in joyful memory
of Michael Stocking

Contents

Acknowledgements

A huge thanks to Abi Malortie, Kate and Derek White, Simon and Hattie Baker, Jennie Pollock, Lloyd and Katherine Porter and Sheila Thomas who have helped so much in producing this book.

Introduction

We start making decisions early.

The Jesuits tell a joke about a discerning mother who goes to her local priest to ask advice. 'Father,' she says, 'I have a little boy who is six months old. And I am curious as to what he will be when he grows up.' The priest says, 'Place before him three things: a bottle of whiskey, a dollar bill and a Bible. If he picks up the whiskey, he will be a bar tender; if he picks up the dollar bill he will be a banker; and if he picks up the Bible he will be a priest.' The mother thanks him and goes home. The next week she returns. 'Well?' says the priest, 'Which one did he pick up: the whiskey, the dollar bill, or the Bible?' She says, 'He picked up all three!' 'Ah,' says the priest, 'A Jesuit!'

I don't know that much about Jesuits but I was making life-changing decisions when I was twelve. I moved school without my mother knowing it when I was fourteen. I chose my lifetime professional path when I was fifteen, then left home when I was eighteen to make it all happen. There have been many mistakes, misunderstandings, tight spots and muddles along the way. Rash acts of foolishness, selfish agendas and falling into holes I should have noticed have all been present. But failure has been the great teacher we all know it is, particularly if we take time to notice what happened and ask why it went wrong.

One of the most successful men in corporate history was brilliant at work but did not seem capable of transferring that brilliance to a critical area of his personal life. The cofounder of Apple and CEO of the company until his death in 2011 was Steve Jobs, and I enjoy and inhabit the 'i' world he created. For whatever reason wisdom seemed to desert Jobs when it came to making decisions about food and health. Having been diagnosed with operable cancer Jobs instead turned to therapies that did not help. In his biography Walter Isaacson explains that to the dismay of those who loved him, Jobs decided surgery was not an option for him.[1] He seems to have placed his hope on a strict vegan diet, many glasses of carrot juice, fruit juice, acupuncture and a psychic. Who knows what would have saved his life, but delaying surgery to explore other remedies seems to have been significant in Jobs succumbing to cancer at 56.

We all need to cultivate wisdom. Great decisions emerge out of wisdom's rich soil. This is the theme of *Wisdom Road*. Regardless of whether you are a Jesuit, a legendary culture changer like Steve Jobs or an ordinary person living an ordinary life, we all need help in cultivating wisdom.

Most mornings, over the last ten years, I have prayed this prayer:

The night has passed, and the day lies open before us; let us pray with one heart and mind. As we rejoice in the light of your presence, O God, set our hearts on fire with love for you; now and forever.[2]

This is a *Wisdom Road* morning prayer that often sets me up for the day. Every morning it teaches me that 'the night is past,' so yesterday is gone and I need to realise this afresh. 'The day lies open before us,' the future is today and right now, so my choices in the next moments are critical. 'Pray with one heart and mind,' so I need to pull my heart and mind together in one place. 'As we rejoice,' I need to make a decision to choose joy right now. 'In the light of your presence,' I will live today in the luminous presence of God. 'Oh God, set our hearts on fire with love for you now and forever,' I am dependent on God setting his burning love in my heart today and the rest of my life.

This is a prayer for those who want to be on *Wisdom Road*. What do I need to pay attention to so I can live well as I walk down *Wisdom Road*? That is what the rest of this book is about. There are three critical areas we will explore: discernment, decision-making and transition. What is decisive in developing discernment? What needs attention when I am making a decision? How do I move on to the rest of my life?

The desire driving *Wisdom Road* is not that perfect decisions will be made. This is not a 'how to make a perfect decision' book. I want to point out the things we need to notice before making a decision and some of the critical things happening in the middle of decision-making. Before you go to the North Pole it is good to see what could possibly be ahead so you know what to take on the journey. I also want to provide a place to come back to when a decision does not work out as you planned. When things don't work out we need to notice what we missed, re-gather ourselves around the things that matter, and have another go. Paralysis, passivity and self-pity are not options. Decisions that don't work out can be wonderful if we know how to handle them well. All of what is ahead has been helpful for me and I am a fully paid-up member of the vulnerable and dim club.

Time to put the boots on. We are heading down *Wisdom Road*, the most stimulating and enriching road of all. Why is it so good? It is the road to fresh discovery and new understanding and is right at the core of a well lived life.

PART ONE

Four Foundations for Discernment

We are slowly drowning, sucked under and weighed down by images and data. We are being flooded by cascading amounts of information about us and in us. More information is gurgling through our heads, hearts and conversations than those of any generation before. We have the ability to know something about almost everything, but find ourselves in crisis. After many conversations with people seeking to find the best route for their lives I believe our crisis is that, with all our information and data, we are losing our capacity to discern and decide. We are alive, yet seem stunned and numbed at the same time. Our data tsunami has helped us participate in an exponential increase in knowledge and cleverness, but has been combined with a catastrophic collapse in discernment and wisdom.

We know much about the techniques of living. We know how to make money – don't spend it unless you have to, and keep investing the excess if you have some.

We know about the techniques of romance – pay attention, focus, and find your partner's love language. We know how to get what we want – set your goals, work hard, network and don't quit. Yet, we have forgotten how to live. We have forgotten how to build our lives through wisdom, and have settled for developing quick and clever techniques to get us through. How can we avoid drowning in information, so that we can float in wisdom? What can move us on from this crisis? The answer is contained in one word – discernment.

What do I mean by discernment? It is the ability to separate, sift and distinguish, so that we can be all we are intended to be. Jesus talked of this discernment using a startling phrase when He said, 'Therefore be as shrewd as snakes and as innocent as doves.'[3] He was saying be wide awake but pure, and be 'switched on' yet without guile. Here Jesus puts together two powerful yet beautiful images of a discerning person – be a snake and be a dove. You do not learn how to become a discerning 'snake-dove' by accident. You have to be trained. You have to learn.

Does it matter if you are not a discerning person? The cost can be high if you do not develop a heart inclined towards wisdom. You borrow money when you can't pay it back, you enter into relationships that end in train wrecks, you grasp for things that you shouldn't, and imagine things are real when they are just passing daydreams. I have done all of these things at one point or other but never all at once... yet.

John was an unmarried priest I knew a few years ago. In our conversations I asked him how he dealt with sexual temptation as a celibate male. He said, 'I pray.' 'What do you pray?' I asked. He said, 'Well, when it comes to sex there are times when I have the opportunity and there are times when I have the inclination. My prayer is that I never have the opportunity when I have the inclination.' The rewards are high if you can work through the tangled reality of human existence and see what is going on.

Does discernment matter to great people? Yes, indeed. In his better days, Solomon prayed for himself as he faced the responsibility of national leadership, 'So give your servant a discerning heart to govern your people and to distinguish between right and wrong.'[4] Paul prayed for the Philippians this remarkable and insightful prayer:

> And this is my prayer: that your love may abound more and more in knowledge and depth of insight, so that you may be able to discern what is best and may be pure and blameless until the day of Christ, filled with the fruit of righteousness that comes through Jesus Christ – to the glory and praise of God.[5]

The Psalms begin with a warning, insisting that we need advice and help to be 'like a tree planted by streams of water, which yields its fruit in season and whose leaf does not wither – whatever they do prospers.'[6] Love, knowledge, insight, discernment, purity and a fruitful life are Paul's desires for the people he loves. James says,

> But the wisdom that comes from heaven is first of all pure; then peace-loving, considerate, submissive, full of mercy and good fruit, impartial and sincere. Peacemakers who sow in peace raise a harvest of righteousness.[7]

Jesus gave us a description of the blessed and discerning life in his nine 'blessed' statements. It is difficult to translate the word 'blessed' but the Greek word it is translated from, *makarios*, means content, happy, balanced, harmonious and fortunate.[8] This is my state of being when I know my place in the world and am satisfied with that place. So *makarios* are the poor in spirit, those who mourn, the meek, those who hunger and thirst for righteousness, who are merciful, who are pure in heart. *Makarios* are the peacemakers, those who are persecuted because of righteousness and those who are ill-treated because of their relationship with Jesus. Discernment is right at the heart of a rich, meaningful life and Jesus describes what that life can look like.

How do you acquire a discerning life? This gift of discernment is a most precious gift, but you can't purchase it like a car or a bag of peas. However, it can be cultivated. If you are able to cultivate discernment, much pain can be avoided, and a great, yet challenging, life encountered. This does not mean an easy life, because with discernment comes increased responsibility. Yet if you want to remain a self-enclosed baby for the rest of your life, this sort of discernment will never be yours. I have known a considerable number of adult babies. Discernment is a gift and should not be wasted. It is much more important than sports, owning your own home, the latest model car, designer clothing, international travel, nationality, perfume, your new kitchen or culinary excellence. Our futures depend on discernment. The future of the world depends on it.

In Matthew 7, through a simple yet brilliant story, Jesus lays down four foundations for discernment. What does He say?

Therefore everyone who hears these words of mine and puts them into practice is like a wise man who built his house on the rock. The rain came down, the streams rose, and the winds blew and beat against that house; yet it did not fall, because it had its foundation on the rock. But everyone who hears these words of mine and does not put them into practice is like a foolish man who built his house on sand. The rain came down, the streams rose, and the winds blew and beat against that house, and it fell with a great crash.[9]

Here, Jesus gives us four foundations for a discerning life, the under-structure on which we can build our lives. What are these four foundations? Walk the road with Jesus; anticipate the weather; pay attention to your heart and practise hospitality. It is to these themes we now turn.

Walk with Jesus

*'It is disadvantageous for us to treat God as a
negotiator, both because God needs nothing we have
and because God asks more than we could ever give.
If all things come from God we can see that it is also
unwise to treat God as a negotiator.'*
Miroslav Volf, *Free of Charge*[10]

*'Therefore everyone who hears these words of
mine and puts them into practice is like a wise man
who built his house on the rock.'*
Matthew 7:24

Grace and truth

The foundation of Christian discernment is Jesus; who
He is, what He has done, and what He is doing. He
is the Rock, the Prophet, the Priest and the King. He
is Son of God, Son of Man, the second person of the
Trinity and the Word. You don't get Christian discernment unless you get Him. To live a life of wisdom, and
encounter the discernment which flows from it, requires
a life built on, in and through Jesus Christ. Our primary
gift, wonder and glory is Jesus Christ. He is the compass
of the future and the nourishment for the present. He
is the bright and morning star, the one who shines out
above all others in His brilliant, captivating splendour.
He is our daily bread, living water and the door through

which we encounter everything good. Our short- or long-term emotional, social and spiritual health do not primarily depend on the stock market, pension fund managers or decisions made by business, political or social leaders. Our futures depend on the way we engage with this Jesus Christ.

There is a description of Jesus in the book of John, 'We have seen his glory, the glory of the one and only Son, who came from the Father, full of grace and truth.'[11] Jesus is the one and only, literally one of a kind. He is unique, and has no equal because He is fully God and fully human. He has no parallel and will never be repeated. Jesus is full of grace and truth. What does this mean?

Jesus told the story of a disobedient, adventurous and prodigal son.[12] He leaves his father, takes his inheritance and heads for wine, women and song. He ends up eating with pigs and, in desperation, finally returns to his father who puts on a huge banquet for this wayward son. The son is brought back into the family. He was lost but now is found. He was dead but now is alive. He receives undeserved, loving, generous grace from the father.

Through this and other stories Jesus was demonstrating the way He works. It is about the remarkable discovery that you have found favour with God even though it was never deserved. This grace is intentional love and focused generosity and it is given to confused, rebellious and messed up people. The story of the prodigal son lets us know that it is possible to change direction and head down a different road.

John says Jesus is also 'true'. He is as straight as an arrow exploding from a bow. He is full of integrity, being pure and whole in every dimension. So, His grace is not some self-indulgence or softness on His part. His grace is full of honesty and correct judgement. When judgement is needed, judgement is delivered. On one occasion Jesus went into a temple and threw out those who exploited others in the name of God. Through His death He broke the back of Satan's kingdom and all centres of evil. Through these and similar events, He was demonstrating that He is not only full of grace, but also full of truth and power. He is the fighter. He is heaven's champion. This is who Jesus is – God and full of grace and truth, yet arrow-straight and tough as steel. He is the foundation and core of a discerning life. We walk down *Wisdom Road* when we walk with Him with one foot raised.

Hear and do

Yet if you want to develop a discerning life, it is not long before the realisation dawns that understanding this is not enough. Our hearts are deceptive, and tend to be their most deceptive when it comes to our response to Jesus. We can see the grace and truth that Jesus is, but prefer to keep Him at a distance. We look at sports stars, royalty and celebrities from a distance. The good thing about them being distant is that they have no effect on us or, if they do, it does not matter that much. We don't have a relationship with them. We have no responsibilities to fulfil in response to their call on our lives. We hope we have control over the way they shape us, if they shape us at all, and we imagine we can switch them off whenever we want. It is possible to respond to

Jesus in the same way. If we relate to Jesus as a sports star, royalty or a celebrity, He may affect us in some sentimental, distant way, but His wisdom and discernment will never characterise our lives. If we keep Jesus at a distance, turning Him into some sort of hero-celebrity, we will ensure our continued spiritual illiteracy.

To develop discernment you have to have an open heart and head, prepared to listen to what God may say to you. Then you listen and listen again. This will take some time and focus to do it well. Then you do what He says. You have not really heard unless you have a go at *doing* what Jesus says. Doing what Jesus says is not as simple as it sounds, but is core to developing a discerning life. What is critical in developing this discerning life? The practices, habits, rituals and routines we live through every day.

Even though we are complex people, full of rich differences and histories, what we do on a regular basis creates much of what we are. We become like what we love and ultimately we are what we love. James K.A. Smith explains how our love is formed in us.[13] He sees the education of our desires being one of our greatest challenges. I think it goes like this: The way in which our loves and desires become what they become is through what fills our imaginations. But before that, our imaginations are formed through our dispositions, and the feelings and attitudes we choose and possess. Yet what forms our dispositions? What are we exposed to through habit and ritual? What do I do on a regular basis most of the time or every day? What I expose my senses to, and where I place my body, will form me into much of what I am. Our imaginations are shaped by all the words and images pouring into our brains through the senses. My love and desire will be shaped by where I put my heart, head and body – by what I do. This is what Jesus was teaching. So our wisdom and discernment are cultivated through hearing and then doing what Jesus says, putting our hearts, heads and bodies into places that cause our love for Him to grow. Love requires no less.

We all love something. The question is: what is it that we love? What does that love achieve in our lives as we pursue it with our time, money and attention? If my love and desire is primarily money, then my heart will become as numb to others as money is. If my primary love and desire is pornography, then my heart's capacity for intimacy will be as unrelentingly stone-cold as pornography is. If my primary love and desire is power, then my heart will become as corrupt as power, when left on its own, ultimately is. So, Jesus says, 'if you love me keep my commandments'. Love Him and desire Him if you want a discerning life.

What do we need to do to put this foundation in the right place?

With the strength, courage and mercy given to us through the Holy Spirit we have to make choices. We have to engage with the practice of saying 'yes' and 'no'. When we realise who Jesus is, and are drawn towards Him, we pledge ourselves to Him. We say 'yes' to Him. In doing this, we shun other possible loves that would take His place. We say 'no' to other idols that are on offer to take His place. A puny response will not do here. We need to say a strong, vivid 'yes' and a ringing, vibrant 'no'. The truth is that we are always saying 'yes' and 'no' in everything we do or do not do, but we might not be conscious of the process. Passion, discipline and action are critical here; the bland and mediocre will not do.

A life of repentance is vital for the development of discernment. This is the process of *metanoia*, the choosing to turn to God. This is at the heart of Christian wisdom and discernment. When we practise repentance we constantly turn to realign our lives with the call of God in us. In the process we discover our true selves in open, full and joyous relationship with God.

To establish this first foundation for discernment, we need to learn to speak 'yes' and 'no'. We need to have supple hearts which are able to turn and run back to the one who made us. Walking with Jesus is the foundation. We start building here.

Anticipate the weather

The early Church believed that its own fragile and vulnerable state was deceptive.
Samuel Wells, *Improvisation: The Drama of Christian Ethics*[14]

The rain came down, the streams rose, and the winds blew and beat against that house; yet it did not fall, because it had its foundations on the rock.
Matthew 7:25

Vulnerability and battering

House building is about a vision of the future. Every nail, floorboard and window is an expression of what you think may take place where you live. Quality house-builders build in a way that anticipates the possible local conditions – all of them. What effect will the sun, rain, wind and cold have on the house? What can be built that will protect the people who live in it? What are the materials needed to make sure this house is able to stand in all possible conditions? These are the questions that every builder has to ask before they start the building project. The critical starting point is the foundations. What sort of underpinning will this house have? Even a beautiful house filled with artistry and decoration is entirely dependent on the solidity of its foundations.

The first house Jesus refers to in this story has strong foundations. He was suggesting that your life be like this house. The rain will come down, the streams will rise and the winds will beat this house. It will be tested. He was saying that this house-building is like life-building – it is a great act of faith. As we build our life-house, we are anticipating our possible futures. The quality of the foundation is a statement about what we think will happen in the future. Jesus was saying to get ready for all weathers – prepare now for all conditions, be they balmy, sunny days or when the rain comes down, streams rise and the wind blows. Prepare for calm conditions and for intense storm. The whole of scripture teaches us that, at some point, we are going to live with turbulence in one form or other. Life after life pays witness to this.

Yet, as you trace the stories of biblical heroes, there is a significant twist. They do go through turbulent conditions, but these very conditions are the material with which their future is built. These bad conditions help them towards their glorious future, rather than deflecting them into self-indulgence or pity. It is as though they take the rain, floods and wind hitting their lives, submit to God and texture it all in to their future. Abraham was called into constant change and a travelling life as he responded, in faith, to God's call. Often it looked like he was living in uncontrollable storm, but really God's house was being built in him and through that, a whole nation. Joseph was put in a hole by his brothers, then sold into slavery, and eventually dumped and forgotten in prison. It looked like he was spiralling down, but really he was being built into a great leader for a critical time. Paul was converted and God's plan for him was to suffer for God's name. It looked like these conditions of suffering would damage him, but this was going to make him into the man he became. Jesus died and it looked like His death was the worst of conditions, but in the middle of the story of loss, Jesus rose from the dead. Jesus taught us this: 'Whoever wants to save their life will lose it, but whoever loses their life for me will find it.'[15] Being ready for all the possibilities of what that might mean is pivotal in the development of a discerning life.

Inner freedom

Discernment is severely diminished if our hearts are not free. If we are not free enough to allow God to bring to us whatever conditions He chooses we easily slip into religious consumerism where we push all the buttons and pull all the levers in selecting the options we think are good for us. This position will always confuse us. Five hundred years ago a Basque priest called Ignatius of Loyola[16] had remarkable insight on this. He described inner freedom as being,

> Where people no longer desire health more than sickness, wealth more than poverty, a long life more than a short life, honour more than dishonour but instead they desire what brings them closer to the end for which they are created.[17]

The idea is that you loosen the controls of your own life. This means that you are free from dictating to God the conditions in which you think you need to live. You leave that to God. If we constantly impose our own will on our own lives we will not be free.

There are two great prayers of inner freedom and outstanding faith that, when prayed, open us up to a discerning life. Firstly, Mary's prayer: 'I am the Lord's servant... May your word to me be fulfilled.'[18] Secondly, the prayer Jesus taught us: 'Your kingdom come, your will be done.'[19] Our requests, tears, shouts and demands to God for Him to do this or that need to be saturated in these huge prayers. We will not be open and free unless that is so and we will not develop a life of discernment.

What do we need to do to put this foundation in the right place?

We have to become familiar with our own story. We need to notice the true nature of our own lives. This means being able to cling to the untidy history and jagged edges of what we have lived through so far. In the initial training of learning how to swim, you are taught to make friends with the water and how to float. This is the best way to avoid drowning. In a similar way we have to learn to make friends with our own lives and notice what God is doing in them. We can do this through keeping a journal in whatever way is best and then regularly reviewing our reflections. Do this honestly and reasonably consistently and you become familiar with your own true story. We can also do this by sharing our story with others. These will be critical in cultivating discernment.

Choosing challenging options prepares us for living in all conditions. If we focus on ease and softness we weaken our ability to discern. If we do not road test our own lives and see what we are like in various conditions, we will not be prepared for the potential storm and subsequent flood. We will not be ready to fight for the oppressed, the poor and the establishment of the Kingdom of God.

Pay attention to your heart

'Understanding and interpreting your emotions is one of the best ways to hear God's desire for your life choices.'

Anon

'But everyone who hears these words of mine and does not put them into practice is like a foolish man who built his house on the sand.'

Matthew 7:26

Jesus explained that the foolish man built his house on sand, choosing not to build on rock. This decision ensured that he, and all who lived in his house, would eventually be overwhelmed. What happened? The wise builder and the foolish builder look much the same. Both were exposed to what Jesus had to say, both received the same opportunity. The critical difference was in implementation. Both heard but only one acted. Both received wisdom, but only one turned this advice into concrete action.

Why would you build your house on sand? What self-deception could lead to such a bad decision? Impatience? Maybe he just wanted the house building to be quick. Superficiality? Maybe he could not be bothered with research. Pride? Maybe he could not take advice from anyone, so chose to go his own way. Money? Maybe he wanted a fast house sale to an ignorant buyer. Image? Maybe his focus was on how it all looked rather than how it all was. Insecurity? Maybe he was competing with the rock builder and wanted to demonstrate his way was faster. Could it be that he just did not know how to build at all and so built on sand out of ignorance and dumbness, failing to understand the implications of what he was doing?

Imagine your heart is a dog and you have put it on its lead and you are taking it for a walk. Where is your dog-heart pulling you on this walk? Is it dragging you along? Is it really the dog taking you for a walk? What is distracting it as you walk? Does it want to fight all the other dogs? Does it want affection? Or possibly it does not want to walk at all and you are dragging it along, while your dog-heart tries to root itself on the road by ploughing its claws into the earth. A distracted heart, a fighting heart, a heart that needs affection and a heart that wants to go nowhere are all metaphors for the condition of our hearts. If you want to know where your heart is and where it will go, you need to identify what you treasure. 'For where your treasure is, there your heart will be also,'[20] said Jesus. You open up the treasure chest of your life and discover your heart there.

Emotional life

To be able to develop discernment you will need to become familiar with your emotional life. You will need to track your own heart. Are our emotions useful? The ancient Greeks tended to think we would be better off with *apatheia* or 'apathy' which was freedom from emotions. Kierkegaard disagreed, explaining that the good life was based on passionate inwardness. I am going with Kierkegaard. Emotions give our life meaning;

they let us know what is going on in us and around us. Rather than our emotions being dangerous and to be avoided, they are intelligent, extremely helpful and need to be noticed. To understand your emotions is to understand much of yourself. They are intelligent and can give you a key to the meaning of your own existence. More than that, they are crucial in the way God communicates with us through the voice of the Holy Spirit. To be able to discern well we will need to notice our fear, anger, love, apathy, passion and tenderness and whatever else is passing through our hearts.

The contribution of the previously mentioned Ignatius is dazzling in working out how to track our hearts and hear the voice of God.[21] There are many other schemes, systems and plans for listening to God but Ignatius is the Big Daddy of them all. Ignatius did serious work on how to renew and deepen our relationship with Christ with his invitation to meditate on the Gospels. He understood the spiritual battle behind discernment. If you want a quick fix to deliver a discerning life He will not help. If you want the quick fix, you are already building on sand and the storm clouds are forming in the distance.

Even though throughout the world God is speaking through teaching, preaching, prophetic words, dreams and visions, hearing the voice of God at a deeper level is invariably slow. There are rapid breakthroughs in our life with God but if they are not followed up by routine practices they eventually fade away. It is best to imagine yourself as a tree to be watered, rather than a rocket to be fired or a resource to be deployed. 'God has sped spiritual growth up because we are in a technological age,' I heard one speaker strangely say. I liked the rest of his message but not that line. It is pivotal to be able to slow down and Stephen Cottrell, in the words of the title of his book, learned how to 'Do nothing to change your life.'[22] God is not forced to move at the pace of Microsoft or Google. He can go much faster or much slower. It is still the case that the strong and blessed person is the one 'whose delight is in the law of the Lord, and who meditates on his law day and night. That person is like a tree planted by streams of water, which yields its fruit in season and whose leaf does not wither – whatever they do prospers.'[23]

What do we need to do to put this foundation in the right place?

Meditation on, and contemplation of, scripture is critical in the development of your own inner life. There is no substitute or short cut to developing discernment. Reading, hearing, meditating and praying scripture has no equal in your spiritual formation. This is where we learn who God is, who we are, what is going on in the world and what we should be doing. It is through scripture that God's word comes to us and we are able to discern what is upside down and right way up. It is only as scripture is woven into our hearts that we can begin to track what is going on deep down inside. It is scripture that challenges us and pulls our imaginations back into the right shape. Pray for and cultivate a love for the Bible if you want discernment. Then get yourself into a regular pattern of reading and meditation that will go on until the end of your days.

Solitude and silence are desirable but not always easy to create. The demands of contemporary life, the data swamp and our high aspirations get in the way of solitude and silence. Solitude does not mean loneliness and silence does not mean dullness. In solitude and silence we are in the company of Father, Son and Holy Spirit. You are never alone in this sort of solitude. Sometimes fear keeps us away from solitude and silence because we are just scared of what we might have to deal with when we listen. But facing that fear is just part of the process of growing up. It will also mean that we will need to be free enough to not have a full diary. This is a place of high anxiety for many because being busy is one of our tribal markings of so-called success. Why are these practices important? In solitude and silence we are saying to God our time is yours and we are ready to listen. They become places of revelation, but you have to hang around with God to get them, and He is in charge of when they come.

Practice hospitality

*Shine, from the inside out that the world might see
you live in me.*
All-age worship song by Nick Jackson

The wise man built his house upon the rock.
Matthew 7:24

Building for others

House building is about others. It is about establishing a place where you can bring up a family, offer hospitality, be safe and participate in the wider community. It is also about making a village, town or city. Building a house is much more significant than the personal agenda of the builder. If you are the house builder, then your responsibility is the safety of all the people who will live there for the next twenty years. You must think long-term and you must think of other people. This is why building on sand is not just a mistake but can also be a sin, particularly if you have been warned to build on rock. Building on sand, when you have been told to build on rock, is an act of negligence.

It can come as a shock when you discover you are not the point of your own life. This is the point when all the walls of self-enclosure, that you might not know are even there, begin to slowly crumble or come crashing down in a flood. The discovery that you are living a self-enclosed life can stop you in mid-sentence or creep up on you slowly like a stalking cat. However it comes, this revelation is central to developing discernment. I often feel a vague sense of desperation when meeting an older person who has never discovered this. It is surely a significant failure if you reach your forties still believing you are the sun around which everyone else must revolve. The reality is that we are all part of a huge saga. Our houses are parts of towns, towns are parts of cities and cities are submerged into countries and eventually the world. The saga is the long story of all the rich and often complicated events taking place in the life of a community and a nation.

The wise man built his house on the rock. He was building his house so it would be a place where others could live over the long haul. He was building part of a town which was interconnected with every other house in the area. House building, like life building, is a social event and everything in scripture points to that being true.

Outside yourself

Our self-absorption will rob us of discernment. Self-absorption prevents us from seeing. It is like being at a football match trying to watch the game with some loud hulk in front of you constantly standing up and blocking the view. In self-absorption this hulk is inside your own head and heart so you cannot see what is happening outside the borders of your own life. You can't see the game. Self-absorption is also like having a series of mirrors encircling your own head with the reflection sides all turned inward. It is impossible to see beyond them because you are always the largest thing you can see. You fill your own vision. With these mirrors in place it is impossible to enter self-forgetfulness which is so important in discernment. Self-forgetfulness is a place which not only cultivates discernment but is the place of deep, deep joy.

How do we know if we are self-absorbed? Three questions will constantly fill our minds and shape our response, even though we might not be aware that we are asking them. Question one is 'Am I right?' Question two is, 'Am I safe?'[24] Question three is, 'Am I happy?' If those questions dominate our heads and hearts it will be difficult to develop a healthy life and cultivate discernment. We will need to get beyond these questions so we can ask other more interesting and important questions that are much more to do with 'we' and 'us' rather than 'me' and 'I'. We develop discernment if we can see outside of ourselves and focus on the world around us. Rather than this depleting us, the opposite happens. We begin to see our own lives in the middle of other lives. We learn that we are part of a wonderful complex pattern of humans. Wisdom and discernment begin to pour in at that point because our vision is not blocked by our own self-love.

What do we need to do to put this foundation in the right place?

First, we must love the Church. If we are going to live from the inside out we need to pray for an increasing hunger to love the Church. For all of her confusions and contradictions the Church is the most beautiful of creations. She is the most beautiful of all in the world. She consists of people made in the image of God who want to live the best they can for the one who made them.[25] Such wonders happen in church. People forgive other people. People have patience with other people. People encourage other people. People heal other people. People rejoice with people. People suffer with people. People give to people. The Church is a wonder because she displays the wonder of God. Certainly there is sin, fear and hypocrisy but the overwhelming majority of the Church consists of earnest people seeking to live the best they can. I know this to be true. I have spent thirty years travelling the world speaking and interacting with churches of all sorts and she is wonderful. Jesus loves the Church, and discernment comes to those who love what Jesus loves.

Second, we must get out and love the world. Archbishop William Temple famously said, 'the church is the only co-operative society in the world which exists for the benefit of its non-members.' This is probably an exaggeration, but it is an insightful line. Wonderful as the Church is, we have not always loved the world well. Apartheid, racism, misogyny and a bias towards the rich have brought much hurt and still do. We cannot change the world by ourselves, but we can change our world through one prayerful act at a time. Acts of loving service to our local, national or global world will cultivate discernment in us like nothing else can. You learn so much through investing in the bank of service to others. This brings us back to our first foundation. We hear and then do if we want to develop discernment. If you want discernment turn your attention to the world and work out how you can love and serve the people in it.

Consequences of discernment

'When Jesus finished saying these things the crowds were amazed at his teaching, because he taught as one who had authority and not as their teachers of the law.'
Matthew 7:28-29

As I said earlier, to construct a house of discernment, walking with Jesus is foundational along with anticipating the weather, paying attention to our hearts and practicing hospitality. If these things become foundational for our lives, increasing wisdom, insight and discernment will result. On the other hand, there is another way to live. If we choose to walk away from the God who made us, insist we get our own little way, ignore the condition of our inner life and expect that the world serves us, we cultivate a different life. Oblivion is often the result.

People loved what Jesus said. They were amazed at this house building story. Why was that? It was because He spoke with authority. He spoke from wisdom, demonstrating His discernment, and that gave Him influence. Discerning people are attractive to people hungry for truth and freedom. Grow in wisdom and discernment and people are drawn to you if they want to know how to live well. But His authority was not only rooted in His words, but also in His deeds. They listened to Him because His life was one confluence of word and deed as He displayed His wisdom and power through His discerning life. He taught them how to live and He teaches us as well. He is working with us as we battle our way through the data swamp, media flood and the collapsing walls of contemporary culture. He teaches us so we can sift, distinguish and discern enabling us to walk out of dark ignorance and into wisdom's brilliant light. This sets us up for decision-making, to which we now turn.

Part One questions

Do you know a wise and discerning person? How do you think they became this way?

What do you think you can do to develop a wise and discerning heart?

In what way are your emotions helpful in developing discernment? In what ways could they be unhelpful?

Cynicism, naiveté, ignorance and arrogance get in the way of cultivating discernment. How can you avoid these characteristics?

What place does prayer play in developing discernment?

Are you aware of evil forces working against you as you seek to follow Jesus by doing what He told you to do? Why do you think that is? How can you address this?

PART TWO

Decision Making

Discernment is critical as we walk down *Wisdom Road*. Our lives are made up of thousands upon thousands of decisions that emerge from our capacity to discern. Most of these decisions seem insignificant and instinctive at the time, but all of them gather together and make a life. In the middle of these tiny choices are deliberate and significant decisions that turn the course of our lives in a totally different direction. Where shall I live? Shall I marry? What job shall I take? Do I take that bribe? Will I choose bitterness? Will I assume my life is all about me? These are just some of the big questions around which we make our decisions. *Wisdom Road* is about the decisions we make and how we build, or possibly dismantle, our lives through these choices.

Our mundane decisions reveal what is happening in our hearts. The jokes we tell, the compassion we show, the disposable cash we spend, the looks on our faces and the words we speak reveal the judgements we have made regarding whatever we have just been confronted with. Much of our decision-making comes out of where our hearts have fed while we munch through the mundane routine of our own lives. As the Dominicans say, 'What is contemplated leads to everything else.'

We don't always age well. Some age cultivating barbed wire hearts. Anger and cynicism bleed from our hearts often noticed by others. The barbed wire heart can sometimes be traced back to idealism that was betrayed and a decision that did not work out as planned. Idealism believes that if you make the *right* decision and do the *right* thing you will get what you want. This is highly unlikely. Yet often, if patient, we may eventually thank God that the decisions made did not work out as originally planned. Richer and better things emerge that our hearts could never imagine if we are able to cultivate soft, teachable hearts.

How do you learn to make a good decision? Usually by making bad ones and learning from them. That process produces humility followed by experience which then kicks on into wisdom. To make good decisions we need to swim in wisdom's sea. It is one of the greatest needs of our time. Christian scripture is full of wisdom. Wisdom is right at the tips of our fingers as we turn the pages and read the stories of Abraham, Moses, Sarah, Esther, Peter, Mary, Paul and Jesus. If these stories start to shape your heart, they become instinct. They often let you know what you should do.

Good decision

She emerged out of a conference. Hundreds were there but she stood out. Other attractive women were distracting but I was drawn to her. I first noticed the emotional poise and athletic body but not in that order. She walked with casual ease. Each limb was speaking to the other in co-ordinated conversation. She had a gentle, slightly rolling walk. She was Canadian, interesting, intelligent and had a face that has always fascinated me. We first touched as I helped her across a pool of water one dark, dull night in Istanbul. We touched again as she lay on an Afghan road sick from eating unwashed grapes in the last town. A year later we had a dinner at Harrison Hot Springs hotel in British Columbia and as we stood on the jetty going out into the lake I asked her to marry me. A great decision was made. I knew a brilliant deal was done, and the last three decades together have demonstrated this in a-thousand-times-ten-thousand ways.

Poor decision

Ted was a gifted member of the church where I was the Senior Pastor. Ted smiled much of the time and was charming most of the time. He had suffered heavy loss in his family and seemed ready to help anyone. I felt I needed him. I needed back up and was desperate to show the signs of success in a critical project. I was sure he was the right man to work with me. Ted's previous church leader had gently warned me about him but I either did not pay attention or just thought he was wrong. Ted said yes to my invitation but, once in post, he changed. The deterioration in our relationship was so quick I was stunned. I have heard of brides sensing the disintegration in their relationship with the newly acquired husband as they walked back down the aisle after marriage. A similar thing had happened to me with my new colleague. I was in disorientated tailspin, wondering how this relationship would land. I had made a poor decision and knew this was a deal I had to exit, and exit I did. After a while we discovered that there were problems in Ted's life that had been unclear to me. The considerable complications he was living through meant he had to distance himself from his church leader. I should have listened to his previous church leader but did not.

Our lives are made of these sorts of decisions. They are the choices that form the rest of our lives. These decisions, at best, are the doors through which we walk into a new room full of wonderful experience. At worst, they are the doors into a prison and we spend our time desperately seeking to get out if we could just find the door again.

Decision one: Henri Salmide

No choice I have ever made has come close to the decision made by Henri Salmide, who died on 23 February 2010. He was a petty officer in the German Navy. He began life as Heinz Stahlschmidt. He defied his officers and became a French hero. Heinz was an expert in demolitions and in 1944 was ordered to prepare the seven miles of French docks for destruction. The US 3rd Army had swung southwards and the American and French forces had landed from the Mediterranean on the Cote d'Azur. He decided to blow up the bunker containing the explosive ordnance instead.

His task in the demolition plan was to lay out the explosives being assembled in a munitions depot close to the port and prepare the fuses so that in one colossal explosion, the port facilities would be unable to function for many months. On August 22 – four days before the scheduled destruction of the port – he laid strips of dynamite inside the munitions bunker and detonated thousands of pounds of explosives in a blast that shook the city by its force. About 50 German soldiers died – something he would have wished to avoid – but he saved the lives of an estimated 3,500. Speaking after the war he said, 'My family were Huguenots and I acted according to my Christian conscience. I could not accept the port should be wantonly destroyed when the war was clearly lost.'[26] He was very popular in France but not so welcome in his native Germany. He lost his military pension.

Decision two: Mountain Madness

One of the most powerful examples of flawed decision-making is the 1996 Mount Everest tragedy. The story is explained in *Into Thin Air* by Jon Krakauer, and commented on by Michael Roberto.[27]

Two expedition teams were caught in a storm, high on the mountain, on 10-11 May 1996. Both team leaders along with three team members died during the storm. The two teams – *Mountain Madness*, led by Scott Fischer and *Adventure Consultants*, led by Rob Hall – were commercial expeditions, meaning that the individuals were paying clients who were to be guided by the professionals to the top.

It is difficult to climb Everest. It has been described as like running on a treadmill while breathing through a straw. One of the rules of climbing Everest is the turnaround time rule. The rule is that if you cannot reach the top by 13:00 or 14:00 then you turn around, because you do not want to be climbing down in darkness. Some of the team members on this expedition arrived after 16:00. In his book *Into Thin Air* Jon Krakauer says, these turnaround times were egregiously (flagrantly) ignored. On their way down the teams were hit by a raging blizzard and five people died high on the mountain.

Why did these men die? The answer is complex, as it is difficult to know exactly what happened on the mountain, but as Roberto explains, given the story it seems that several biases played their part: overconfidence, sunk-cost and availability.[28] What are these biases?

Overconfidence bias

We make poor decisions because we are overconfident in our own ability to assess and understand a situation. In this bias we believe we can do what we cannot do. It seems that the leaders of these expeditions were just overconfident. Scott Fischer, the leader of *Mountain Madness*, explained that he thought they had mastered Mt. Everest and that it was as easy as walking down the famed Yellow Brick Road of *The Wizard of Oz*. When one climber was worried about the team's ability to reach the summit, Rob Hall expressed that they had done this climb 39 times, even with people as pathetic as the questioner. They had arrived at a point of very positive self-assessment. Krakauer described them as clinically delusional.

How difficult this can be. In our attempts to be positive and move forward with faith and optimism, how can we discern the moment when our positive attitude merges into some dumb visit to arrogant overconfidence?

Sunk-cost bias

This is the tendency for people to escalate commitment to a course of action in which they have made prior investments of time, money and resources. This is when we 'throw good money after bad'. It is the gambler's bias. It is the bias that kicks in when you look at your car and wonder if the mechanic's suggestion of a new engine is a good idea or not. After consideration you decide 'yes' because you put a new gear box in last year, but may not notice that other parts of the car are deteriorating badly because you have invested so much already. On Everest in 1996 each climber had paid thousands of dollars and spent many months in training and preparation. They had sunk recourses of all kinds into this venture. Having invested so much they invested a little more and that caused their deaths.

Christian leaders are particularly vulnerable to the 'sunk-cost bias' because we begin our building projects and start our programmes with the idea that 'this is what we believe God has told us to do'. Once you have made that statement to your church or team, it is very difficult to step away from it and know the point where you should announce closure and head for the door.

Availability bias

The 'availability bias' is when we tend to put too much emphasis on information and evidence that is most readily available to us when making a decision. You can get fooled by a recent hot streak. David Breashears explains that several periods of good weather had lulled the guides into a false sense of security. He knew that in the mid-eighties – before Hall or Fischer had been on Everest – there were three seasons of ferocious storms that prevented anyone from climbing. He explains that season after season Hall and Fischer had wonderful weather on summit day. They had never been caught in a storm on the mountain.

If you are from an optimistic Christian tradition you can be particularly vulnerable to this bias. The enemy plays it well and you can often see 'the serpent's tail' slipping into the grass but don't quite catch what is going on. It goes something like this, you are in a decision-making dilemma and wondering what to do. Then someone gives you a prophetic word that triumphs over all the experience and wisdom you have gathered through your life. A weak decision follows because you put more value on the recent 'prophetic word' than all the other things God has taught you through hard-won experience and you fall flat on your face. Listening to what God is saying *now* is essential, but all the weight should not be placed on the last word. It usually can't take the weight placed on it if disconnected from the rest of your life and community.

It is possible to make a wrong decision in the same way that Scott Fischer and Rob Hall did. Overconfidence in your own ability to manage your own life; pride because of investment that you can't let go of and a combination of ignorance and inexperience can prevent you from living the life you were called to live.

Where do decisions come from as we walk down *Wisdom Road*?

There are three movements and questions we need to be aware of in decision-making. What is being delivered to us? What is happening in us? What flows out from us? There are no neat lines between these three overlapping areas but they do help to explain what we need to pay attention to as we make decisions. In the decision-making process we are seeking to avoid naïveté and gullibility on one hand and bitterness and cynicism on the other. Our goal is decisions that are wise, challenging and free so that we can be all we should be so that the brokenness of the world is addressed.

Movement One:
Delivered to Us

*The heart is deceitful above all things and beyond
cure. Who can understand it?*
Jeremiah 17:9

There are conditions that have been delivered to us. They roll over us like huge weather systems and we have no choice in their arrival or the time of their departure. This is all the stuff of life that you have to deal with whether you like it or not. I am English, male, tall and born in the middle of the 20th century. All of that came to me. I did not select it or desire it. It was just there. These conditions are the seas we swim in and the lands we live in. They shape all of our visions because they provide the horizon our imaginations can anticipate. Because they shape our visions, they always shape our decisions. They are the givens we interact with all of the time. If we are going to make good, and even great, decisions it will be because we are aware of the conditions delivered to us and become aware of ourselves through them.

What are these conditions delivered to us?

Culture

The place where we were born, and the values embraced in that place, radically shape the way we make any decisions. This is because our culture delivers to us judgements about what is worthy, worthless or irrelevant.

Each of us has been brought up with certain cultural assumptions. My home town is just north of Liverpool. In Liverpool there is a high cultural value on being witty and sarcastic at the same time. This is one of the joys and curses of coming from my home town. Let me tell you a cultural story. I hurt my knee playing cricket and after a visit to hospital it was bandaged and I was walking with a stick. I was living in Bromley at the time. Bromley is the typical 'southern softie' town if you are from the north of England. As I was limping down Bromley High Street, surrounded by southern softies – as some northerners would feel – a friend from near my home town called to me from across the street, 'How's your leg?' I shouted back, 'It is fine thanks.' He shouted back, 'it is a shame about your face!'

Is that funny or what? I have told that story to different audiences all around the world. Some people are appalled by it, saying, 'How could he be so cruel?' Others are delighted, saying, 'How quick, clever and witty!' Personally, I loved it. His response was direct and home-town. It was clever, witty and complimentary, admittedly in a twisted sort of way. Taken at face value the words he said were not helpful, but cruel. But if you come from where I come from, it was quick-witted, loving genius. It was man-talk. I can still feel the smile on my face when he said it.

The culture we are immersed in is always influential because it blinkers us on one hand and gives us telescopic vision on the other. Our culture sets up our value system, and unless challenged in some way, it remains the value system we have for the rest of our lives. Being mentored on the playing fields of Eton will produce a different set of values and decisions than being brought up selling sugar cane on the streets of Mumbai. So, how have we been shaped by our culture and how has that formed our decision-making?

Community

Our cultures are made up of communities and families. These communities are part of the wider culture but they don't share all the same values. Each community is shaped by, and shapes, the wider culture. This is the rich and challenging tapestry of life. We are all brought up in some community, be it brilliant, boring or woeful. If the Italian Mafia was your shaping community – like it was for Frank Sinatra – it is likely you will arrive at the task of decision-making with a different set of ideas than if you were brought up by Christian German Mennonites. Yet beware, because although this is generally true, you cannot always be sure, as there are other things that shape your heart and mind regardless of the community or family from which you emerge.

What kinds of people have shaped your life? Who are the people influencing you today? What has filled their imaginations? How does the company you have kept, and now keep, sway the nature of the decisions you make? If we have just hung around with white, British, middle-class, Anglican charismatics or with American Baptist fundamentalists we will begin to make decisions that reflect the values of these groups. Our decision-making will take on another shape if we are nurtured by the cyber community and live in a world of pretend friends, fantasy games or internet gaming. These communities are very powerful and sometimes subtle in their effects on us. We can't always see how they influence us because we are embedded in them, but influence us they do. These communities pick us up and deliver us to our future through forming the basis upon which we make decisions.

Story

Tied up with my culture and community is my story. Each of us has a story and you usually discover what it is when explaining it to others. When mentoring people I often ask them to write their story. It is always illuminating both for them and for me. As you read most of these stories they are filled with parents, siblings, passions, joys, significant events, questions and troubles. You are able to see what their journey has been as you read the story. Has this person's journey been uphill or dry desert? Has it been smooth waters and flower-filled meadows? How has their story shaped them?

We are living our own story and that story has come out of our gene pool, family relationships, burdens, values, sufferings, visions and the decisions we have made or endured. So, what is my story and what does it mean? What is the story I am living through? What is my history and how does it shape my vision of the future, if I have one?

Critical in the decision-making process is your story. I teach leaders all around the world. Leaders who do not know their own story tend to be victims in one way or another. This is true for each of us. We become victims to busyness, popularity, deception and self-centeredness if we are unfamiliar with our own story. Why? Because when faced with temptations or poor options we have no ability to say, 'this is not me, I won't do that, this is not my story'. If we don't understand our own story, we will go with anything that appears to work and bring 'success'. Henri Salmide knew his story well and it shaped the decisions he made. He was a Huguenot and as far as he could see Huguenots did not blow up docks and waste thousands of lives unnecessarily. You need to know your story, and what it has given you, if your decisions are going to be free from mysterious forces that confuse. If you know your story, you are much better placed to have a great story that brings life to yourself and others through the decisions you make.

Your story will shape you and your decisions. So you need to be aware of the way your story influences those decisions. Ralph was born in poverty, to an alcoholic mother and a philandering father who changed his religious affiliation regularly. Being both intelligent and focused, Ralph did well and became a successful businessman. Yet he never knew the impact of his own story on his decision-making. The luxury boat he bought and kept in the south of France, and the invitations to his family to visit him on his boat, were not simple and free choices. The boat and all the other symbols of success were a reaction to the deprivations and shame of childhood, but he did not know it. Almost everyone else did.

There is a wonderful process of change that can take place if you let God curve into your story. This change may take a while but it is still wonderful. If we open up our lives and allow Him to introduce us to ourselves, we can see how our story has shaped us and what God can do as He enters with forgiveness, mercy, love and grace. Enter into God's great story and have your own story transformed along with the decisions you make. Ralph became a 'born again' Christian but for whatever reason never really let God into his story. Consequently, his decisions often looked weird and insecure.

Frameworks

We all have some sort of decision-making framework in our heads. This is made up of the various beliefs and ideas through which we interpret and interact with the world. These are the ideas and models working away in our heads when we are saying, 'yes,' 'no', 'wait,' and 'maybe.' Some of our basic responses to the world get formed, framed and answered through these sets of ideas working away inside our heads. Is there a God? Is there a Devil? Is the world God's or is it the Devil's? So is the world a place to run towards or run away from? How we answer these, and many other similar questions, will shape the decisions we make, but they will all emerge from the frame inside our heads and hearts that has been shaped by culture, community and our story.

The framework of our decision-making is related to the images and thoughts going through our heads. Each person has a different framework for decision-making. However, there are some large frames which can shape the decision we make. Let me mention four significant ones:

SLAVE FRAME

Inside this frame we feel like slaves or captives. With the 'slave' frame inside our hearts and heads we feel helpless, incompetent and worthless. This often leads to blaming someone else for our imprisonment and all the difficulties we are in. We have become victims of self-inflicted assault. We don't realise that our captivity and victimhood is a place of our own choosing. We are not captive to anyone else but captive to the belief system in our own heads.

SCARCITY FRAME

Inside this frame we can feel empty, anxious and poor, even though we have ample provision and luxury. Both millionaires and people with no money can have this frame in their heads. A friend of mine insists that he does not feel 'safe' unless he has US$ 400,000 in his current bank account. All of his money has not addressed his 'scarcity' frame and the fear that lies behind it. This frame prepares us for a life of taking rather than giving. We always want to hoard but can never gather enough to satisfy our inner need to feel safe.

SON-DAUGHTER FRAME

Inside this frame we feel we have value. The value comes through a permanent, loving, deep and committed relationship with God and others which sets us free. Inside this frame 'success' or 'failure' are less significant because of the overwhelming presence of love right at the centre. Popular definitions of 'success' or 'failure' are not the centre of this relationship. If you live inside this 'Son-Daughter' frame you can make decisions that look risky, or even dumb, but it does not matter that much because the point of your life is the relationship and not being a 'success' or 'failure'.

ABUNDANCE FRAME

Inside this frame we understand and feel personal abundance. We are in a place of always being ready to give, even though it may not look like we have much to distribute. Our culture, community and story have put us in a place where we feel rich on the inside and therefore able to be generous with attention, service, time and talent.

Our culture, community, family, story and frames are delivered to us, but this is not the end because God is at work in re-shaping our histories. God is always on the job of removing our slave and scarcity frames and replacing them with son-daughter and abundance frames.

One thing that has shaped my imagination, and decision-making process, right at the rock face of my own life, is regularly praying: 'Glory be to the Father and to the Son and to the Holy Spirit. As it was in the beginning is now and shall be for ever. Amen.' So much is gathered up in this simple burst of words. They can sink into our hearts and heads, lay there for a while, then explode and shatter our tiny dreams, while at the same time providing the largest frame possible.

Movement Two:
Present in Us

Are you still so dull?...The things that come out of
the mouth come out of the heart.
Matthew 15:16, 18

When making a decision you visit, intentionally or unintentionally, all the rich complexity working away in your own life. You enter the mix of emotions, ideas, relationships, hunger, temptations, visions, defences and articulations of what is inside you. We are a combination of what is given to us, what is present in us and what we choose. This sets up our lives and the decisions we make.

The Challenger Disaster in 1986

After nine years of research, and in her book *The Challenger Launch Decision*, Diane Vaughan gave her explanation as to why the disaster happened.[29] She explained that the primary reason for the tragedy was the normalisation of deviance, or what could be called a slow slide down the slippery slope.

In 1986 the space shuttle *Challenger* was launched. Just over one minute into the flight disaster struck. There was an explosion and all the astronauts were killed. The reason for this tragedy was the failure of two rubber 'O' rings. When the rings failed, hot gasses escaped into the rocket boosters, igniting the fuel. What caused this accident? Flawed human decision-making.

With the wisdom of hindsight we know that the flight should have been delayed, and that if it had, lives would not have been lost. There was a meeting of 34 people the night before the launch; most of them were managers or engineers who were pushing for their own view in a highly combative environment. The decision to launch *Challenger* was taken, even though Roger Boisjoly and some other engineers tried to warn the meeting of the dangers. There had been seven prior incidents of problems caused to the space shuttle due to 'O' ring erosion. Boisjoly presented a chart to the meeting explaining his concerns that the cold weather was likely to have had a serious negative effect on the rubber. In four of the earlier incidents the outside temperature had been between 53°F (12°C) and 65°F (18°C). In the other three incidents the temperature had been above 65°F. The coldest launch took place at a temperature of 53°F, but on the day of the launch of Challenger it was going to be 40°F (4.5°C). From his perspective it was too cold to launch *Challenger*. Boisjoly failed to persuade the meeting, and the launch went ahead.

When the shuttles had been built, the engineers did not expect 'O' ring erosion, but it did happen, even on some successful flights. Eventually some erosion was anticipated, and finally accepted. What was unanticipated became anticipated and eventually merged into the normal. This happened through small deviations slowly being accepted as the norm. It is sometimes easier when exercising to ignore the inconsistent, irritating pain in your chest, but it can be most dangerous if you don't. NASA failed to notice the danger of weak, routine signals indicating there was a problem.

Vaughan explained that the decision to launch was an error rooted in the ordinary process of organisational life. There was no decision to do wickedness. There was rather a series of apparently harmless decisions that eventually culminated in disaster.[30] The people of NASA, like the rest of us, had formed norms, beliefs and attitudes over many years. Vaughan points out that they had huge scheduling pressure, had a culture that emphasised a distinction between managers and engineers, had promoted shuttle flight as routine, and had always operated under the influence of the politics of the day. All of this banal and normal culture was routed into the evolutionary process of NASA that came into play while they listened to, and eventually ignored, Boisjoly.

The decisions we take come out of what we regard as normal, what we believe and the attitudes we possess. They come out of the complex history of what has influenced and formed our heads, hearts and bodies. Therefore it is so easy to begin to slide down the slippery slope and end up with the normalisation of deviance. Did NASA learn? Seventeen years later Columbia burned up while entering earth's atmosphere due to damage caused by another minor failure that had become routine.

The cultures we inhabit, the community where we were formed, the story we have lived and what we believe to be obvious – our frameworks – will shape the decisions we make. But decisions don't just come from what has been delivered to us but from what is present in us.

What are those things present in us that will shape the decisions we make?

Identity

Our decisions come out of who we are. Our decisions are the silvery path left by the snail, and the stream of vapour behind the plane shooting across a blue sky. Our decisions are evidence of what is going on in our lives. They are not the only evidence, but they reveal so much. If my heart is dark and shadowed by unforgiveness, the decisions I make will be characterised by bitterness. If my heart is merciful, baptised in love and grace, my decisions will be characterised by freedom and release, though this does not always come easily. If my life is stuck in the shame of childhood I will make decisions that will try and cover that shame. We pull together the rags of respectability to cover our shame, hoping others will not notice our half-naked state. We put on the manicured nails, toupees, designer labels, uniforms or sparkling personality, but many can see right through the façade as they observe the decisions we make.

Rose, a sport loving Australian woman, has always had difficulty making healthy decisions, partly because she has little knowledge of who she is. Her assumptions are that she is rational, logical, and usually right, and that others are near idiots if they do not agree with her. These assumptions have always muddled her decisions. The reality is that pride, naïveté and self-focus have characterised much of her life, but she has no idea about this identity and its impact on her decision-making. Being in her thirties, Rose's sense of identity is that she is adult, but what others see is an adolescent. Rose needs to be introduced to a new identity and then choose to live out of it. Her marriage and the future of her three children will be shaped profoundly by how her sense of identity develops and the decisions that flow out of it.

Stanley Hauerwas says decision-making is, 'not about what I ought to do but about what I am and ought to be.'[31] Rather than focusing on right or wrong decisions, we need to ask another question – 'Who am I when I make this decision?' Hauerwas goes on to explain, 'The decision makes itself if we know who we are and what is required of us.'[32] Will I slander my work colleague? Of course not, for that is not who I am, I do not slander. Will I give to the poor? Of course, for this is who I am, I seek to be generous with my money. Will I just live for myself? That is impossible because I am not my own to live for myself. Will I seek to love a difficult person? I will because my Lord has asked me to love even my enemies.

Why did Henri Salmide blow up his own German munitions dump? Why did Scott Fischer take such foolish risks on Everest and cause such loss of life? Why did the managers of the space shuttle programme allow *Challenger* to be launched? All of these decisions were an expression of what the decision-makers were; their identity, and not just what they knew. Undoubtedly, there were many complications and complexities in the mix of decision-making, but what they saw themselves to be would have been right at the core of the decisions they made. This is always the case.

How can you find your identity? How can you find out who you are? Identity and love go together. You discover your identity by discovering who and what you love, by discovering who and what you desire. If you are able to find out what you truly love and desire, then follow the line back to your own heart. You will find yourself there.

I have followed football all of my life. The skill of the game, the drama of the match and the intensity of competition has always been compelling to me. It is one of my loves. But for some of my fellow football-lovers it goes much further into cult-like commitment, tribalism and deep, heart-ripping desire. Some Liverpool FC supports sang this song to one of their best players, their captain, Steven Gerrard. If you can imagine the tune of, 'You're just too good to be true' by Andy Williams you will get the feel of this mostly man-to-man sonnet. I have changed the words in italics.

Oh Steven Gerrard – to the tune of 'Too Good to be True'

You're just too good to be true,
Can't take the ball off of you,
You've got a heavenly touch,
You pass like Souness to Rush,
And when we're *drunk* in the bars,
We thank the Lord that you're ours,
You're just too good to be true,
Can't take the ball off of you.

Oh Steven, Steven, Steven Gerrard,
Oh Steven, Steven, Steven Gerrard,
Oh Steven, Steven, Steven Gerrard,
Oh Steven, Steven, Steven Gerrard,
Oh Steven Gerrard

> Because he hates Man U,
> Oh Steven Gerrard,
> He hates the blue *boys* too,
> Oh Steven Gerrard,
> You're a red through and through!

If you can imagine a crowd of over forty thousand (mostly) men, sweating and swaying in a sea of red, in a highly competitive atmosphere and showing much disrespect to their opponents, you will get the power of the song. When asked who they are, many of these supporters' will say, 'I am a Red.' How did they come to being a 'Red' and singing such committed songs? They have been cultivated in being a 'Red.' Their culture, community and story are wrapped up in Liverpool FC. All the success and failure of the team is gathered up into their own identity. They see the world through its frame. It has become a large part, even the dominant part, of their identity.

Although there will be significant areas of our identities that will never change, much can be renovated, renewed and transformed. Our understanding of who we are emerges from history and background, but it can be transformed through Jesus Christ. How does that happen? We receive Him through following Him. The Holy Spirit deposits love for Jesus in our hearts and we are drawn to Him. When the desire is ignited, and we decide to follow, our identities are shaped by practice.

What do I mean by practice? James K. A. Smith nails it with one swing of a solid academic hammer. He explains that our love and desires need to be 'educated' or formed, and he thinks that happens by a combination of practices and routines that instil a particular vision of the 'good life' by allowing that vision into the heart or gut by means of continual practice.[33] In other words, what you do, where you go, what you see and what you touch will form your life. To a large extent, what you practise will decide what you will be when you make a decision. The Church has always known this.

Temperament

I have two great-nieces living in London. The elder one stays on track most of the time. She does not do what she should not do, and is quite sensitive to the boundaries laid around her. The younger is very different. She has been trying to get off track and create her own railway system since the day she was born. When she was almost three she was told by her mother not to bring blossom into the house from the cherry tree in our garden. On receiving this instruction, she picked up as much blossom as a two-year-old can handle and walked to the house, hovering over the entrance between outside and inside. She made sure she had our attention as she tested the boundaries. She held the blossom between the garden and the house and listened to us all say, 'No Alice!' She observed us all getting upset and then dropped the blossom *just* outside, but only so far as to keep her out of trouble. Here are two girls – same parents, environment, town, food and sleeping patterns, but different temperaments. There are no prizes offered for anyone who wants to guess which one is going to take more risks and which will be more risk averse in later life. But we shall see.

There is a long history of temperament study.[34] Most of the schemes seem to break humanity into four categories, but all of them want to help us access our natural predispositions or prevailing mood patterns and work out what they mean as we live our lives. I met one guy for a drink, and after about two minutes of conversation he said to me, 'I guess you are an ENFP.' I was not so ready to be categorised, but he was sure of his analysis. He was referring to the work of David Keirsey's on temperaments, coming out of his book, *Please Understand Me*, written in 1985, and then most famously in the Myers-Briggs personality test.

Are you a Rational, an Idealist, a Guardian or an Artisan? If you are a Rational then you tend to be technical, competent, ingenious, sceptical, innovative and non-conformist. Idealists tend to be romantic, empathetic, authentic, creative and impassioned. If you are a Guardian you tend to be dependable, traditional, and loyal. Artisans are often adventurous, action-orientated, and spontaneous, or so the idea goes.[35]

Occasionally, I have been asked what colour I am. The options are red, blue, white or yellow. I know my colour. We did the Taylor Hartman analysis on our leadership team at church. I am a yellow.

Yellows are motivated by fun. They are inviting and embrace life as a party that they're hosting. They love playful interaction and can be extremely sociable. They are highly persuasive and seek instant gratification. Yellows need to be adored and praised. While yellows are carefree, they are sensitive and highly alert to others' agendas to control them. Yellows typically carry within themselves the gift of a good heart.[36]

Being a yellow means I don't mind telling you all this, or letting you look at the footnote. In fact, I am happy to send you a signed photo of me, and encourage you to visit me on Facebook, listen to my talks online and read my books – which all must be read. I am sure it sounds arrogant and it may be, but I am usually mystified by people who don't like me. I am a yellow.

These temperament categories may or may not be accurate, helpful or even true but they do indicate difference. There were personality differences between Jacob and Esau, Ruth and Naomi and Paul and Barnabas. This sort of difference is celebrated in the book of 1 Corinthians where Paul compares the Church to a body and says we are all like different body parts playing different roles, but part of the one whole.[37] This is vital information when it comes to decision-making.

Some of us are wired for the next big leap into the unknown and others are made to provide the back up for those about to leap. Yet be ready for two twists, because things are not always as they appear on the surface. Twist one is the setting. You can be bold when climbing a mountain but terrified when someone asks you a personal question. You can look timid at a party, while clinging grimly on to your drink – but have a strategy to take on the world. You can be a different sort of person in different settings. Twist two is God's glory. Be ready for God to lead you into something that you consider not to be you because in that place God will receive more glory and you will be of more use.

When it comes to decision-making it really helps if you know how you are made. It helps if you know your nature, but be ready for the twists and turns in the road. In the end we are not Sanguine, Choleric, Melancholic or Phlegmatic[38] but people on a journey to the city of God, and while we travel we work for His kingdom.

Intuition

The life we have lived shapes our decision-making. What have we lived through and what have we learned through that living? What are the frameworks and patterns we have in our heads that have emerged through life experiences? What are the images and mental models around which so much decision-making swings? What decision-making frame has been built in our heads through the experience of life so far?

After the terrorist attack on New York, the 9/11 Commission discovered that many US government agencies were operating in a 'cold war' decision-making frame when the planes hit the Twin Towers and Pentagon. They were living on past experience that had taught them the great threat was another nation state lobbing missiles at them from afar. The 1960s and 1970s were the decades of their primary experience and therefore foundational to their decision-making. They were not ready for the new world of suicide bombers and networks of organisations that crossed national borders.

However, Khalid al Mihdar and Nawaf al Hazimi were well aware of the changes that were taking place and used them to slaughter almost 3,000 people. Past experience had taught some US institutions that the world was a particular type of solid, when in reality it had become fluid.

Drawing too much out of limited experience can cost lives. Remember Scott Fischer, the leader of *Mountain Madness* with his belief that they had conquered Mt. Everest and now it was a benign Yellow Brick Road to the summit? In 1943 Thomas J. Watson is reputed to have said, 'I think there is a world market for maybe five computers.' If he did not say it, others said similar things and understandably so, because there was no experience of what was to come with the microchip. A few years ago I gave my wife a Christmas gift absolutely sure she would not guess what it was. Experience told me I could be sure of this because the gift was so unusual and so well wrapped. I handed it to her saying, 'You will never guess what this is in 120 guesses.' She got it on the first guess. My experience had failed me, my taken-for-granted assumptions needed to be challenged and I clearly could not do it by myself.

The danger with experience is that it blinds as well as enlightens. If we don't humbly bring our experiences into dialogue with other people's experiences it can deteriorate into stubbornness, insularity or even stupidity. Our experiences need to be shared with God and others if we are to reap wisdom from them, enabling us to make great future-shaping decisions. Sometimes we do not understand what we have been through for several decades; occasionally we are never able to understand our experiences at all.

A good friend pulled his car alongside me as I stood by the road. He wound the window down and introduced me to his passenger. I had heard of this man before but never met him. Within the first split second of looking at him there was a negative reaction in me. There was an, 'Oh no,' that registered deep inside, accompanied by a sense of despair. I felt a sense of danger as well. Was I picking up on the words of Nobel Prize winner Daniel Kahneman who wrote that 'survival prospects are poor for an animal that is not suspicious of novelty'?[39] Was it the way he looked or did not look at me? Was it my own mood as I stood by the road? Was it his reputation that I had somehow digested in a negative form? Was it an evil influence tempting and confusing me? Was it the Holy Spirit alerting me? Was it the *Blink* phenomenon, which is, the power of thinking without thinking?[40] Was it intuition? I got to know the passenger in the car, and a few years later I really value that first reaction. It was an over-reaction but it proved to be very helpful in the long run. However, my reactions have not always been so reliable.

Our intuition emerges out of our experience. With intuition we deliberately or accidentally gather millions of fragments of information and store them up in our heads and hearts, then they burst out in a few moments of gut-feeling or insight. Insightful intuition is a gift, a little like linguistic ability.[41] You can't turn your intuition off. There are some who have this gift in abundance and others who do not. However, it is worth remembering that 'the heart is hopelessly dark and deceitful, a puzzle that no one can figure out.'[42] When it comes to decision-making you really can't trust your intuition alone because the corkscrew nature of your own heart can turn inwards and screw you up. As Daniel Kahneman explains, we can be blind to the obvious and blind to our own blindness. But there is a relationship between intuition, gut feeling and the voice of the Holy Spirit. This is so particularly when it comes to prayer: 'In the same way, the Spirit helps us in our weakness. We do not know what we ought to pray for, but the Spirit himself intercedes for us through wordless groans.'[43]

Intuition can be very valuable when put into the family of tools for discernment. However, if you just depend on intuition for making your decisions, you will be doomed to the ignorance of prejudice and follies of foolishness because of your lazy, one-dimensional response to making a decision.

Habits

Slap bang at the centre of the decision-making process will be our practices and habits. Habits are to do with the conditioning of my character, which in turn shapes my decisions. You have more chance of winning the Lottery than making a good decision if these habits are ignored or neglected.

What are these habits? They are not rules for being good; they are the autobahn of a brilliant life. Neither are they about my own little life being lived safely because I am scared of living otherwise; they are the doors which, when opened, lead to luscious virtue. Tom Wright says these virtues 'are, in themselves, the signs of life, the language of life, the life of new creation, the life of new covenant, the life which Jesus came to bring.'[44]

Wright goes on to explain that they are all about the future of the planet and what God has ahead for us. 'God's future is arriving in the present, in the person and work of Jesus, and you can practice, right now, the habits of life which will find their goal in that coming future'.[45] So I can practice now, through my habits and decisions, what is ahead as God opens the future which is indisputably His.

What are these habits which cultivate luscious virtues in decision-making? For me there are five. If I have the time to go through the process – and don't have to make an immediate decision – I always go through a series of questions, either alone or with someone else. The five habits are purity, justice, love, truth and courage. Whatever you can do to cultivate these habits is going to lift the quality of your decision-making. But be warned – they don't always make it easier and they don't guarantee a nice result where everyone feels loved up and wants to dance around the garden once the decision is made. Attempting to live out the values of the Kingdom of God in a broken world can end in crucifixion, as we know.

The five habits become five questions in the process of making a decision:

Question one: Is my heart pure as I make this decision? When you ask yourself this question usually the answer is no. There may well be pride, fear, insecurity and the desire to win which contaminates your motivation. However, we need to face these things and be aware of them in the process. We need to be humbled by our own, occasionally deceptive, hearts. We will need to learn what will be gained or how we will be advantaged through the decision about to be made. There is a need to identify as much as possible your own motivation and face the sometimes brutal reality of the answer.

Question two: Where is the justice in the decision I am about to make? Will justice be served and injustice addressed? Who will be treated unjustly or justly in the decision I am about to make? What will be the result of this decision for the poor, disempowered and disadvantaged? Will I be colluding with forces that dominate and perpetuate injustice?

Question three: Where is love and grace present in the decision I am about to make? By love I don't mean sentimental feelings of romantic love but an act of service when you decentre yourself and put others first. Is this decision a loving act? Who will be loved in this decision and who will be hurt? Will someone else's project, hope or vision get damaged if I do make this decision? Will someone else's project, hope or vision get damaged if I don't?

Question four: Where is truth present in the decision I am about to make? Is what you are about to decide true? Is it true to who you are? It is not always possible to be totally transparent when making a decision. Sometimes others have to be protected and truth becomes concealed because of the necessity of wisdom, but the truth question needs to be explored.

Question five: Am I being courageous in this decision I am about to make? If this question is not asked, there is a possibility you will avoid the decision and become immobile and nailed to the floor by various states of fear. However, courage is a risk so asking this question in conversation with all the other questions is critical.

After going through those questions you will be able to trace the brokenness of your own heart, and realise that without God helping you in the decision, you are entering various stages of doom. This brings us to the subject of sin.

Sin

Sin will always get in the way of making great decisions. It clouds and pollutes, casting a grey mist over everything. But specific sins are not the point here. If you steal, lie and become overwhelmed by jealousy, it will get in the way of making good decisions but those things are symptoms of a deeper problem. The most stunning description of sin I have ever read comes from Stanley Hauerwas when he writes, 'Sin is the form our character takes as a result of our fear that we will be nobody if we lose control of our lives.'[46] Everyone should spend half a day in their favourite place meditating in silence and solitude on this brilliant summation. One month later, take another half day and pray through this additional Hauerwas insight on sin: 'For our sin lies precisely in our unbelief – our distrust that we are creatures of a gracious creator known only to the extent that we accept the invitation to become part of the kingdom.'[47] The truth is we need to let the Holy Spirit work this into our hearts over a number of years, mixed up with tears and many moments of revelation.

The great fundamental sin is not trusting God with our past, present and future. It is our desire to be independent and self-made that messes us up. Like children playing in the sand at the seaside we want to build our own kingdoms and sit on top of them. It is fear of losing our self-made lives, and the need to remain in control, that gets in the way of great decision-making. Much of decision-making is spiritual battle with the world, the flesh and the devil.

The only way to respond to our sin is through the mighty, life-transforming process of repentance. Turning away from our own self-made little lives and casting them at the feet of a loving God is the only way to deal with the sin of seeking life through our own, often pathetic, schemes and devices.

To make great decisions you have to be ready to be changed and willingly slaughter selfish illusions. Only then can you begin to see what is real and what is illusory. We all need help here. How do you slaughter illusions effectively? It often takes wise and courageous company, helping you see what needs to be butchered, along with providing assistance in the direction of the knife.

Imagination

Our imaginations are one of our extraordinary powers and greatest gifts. They give us the power to bring into the present things that are not here. Our imaginations put meaning on everything. With the imagination you can change your history and future for better or for worse. The imagination is at the heart of decision-making. When making a decision it is worth paying a visit to your imagination.

What have I allowed to fill my head and heart? What are the thoughts and feelings that fill my head and heart now? The Dominicans have a saying that captures the power of this: 'It is what is contemplated that leads to everything else'.[48] The continuous contemplation of anything will shape your imagination. In turn this will lead to the rest of your life through the decisions you make.

Private escapist thoughts often break out into public destructive relationships. Private thoughts filled with love often break out in magnificent acts of service. As Paul wrote:

> Therefore, I urge you, brothers and sisters, in view of God's mercy, to offer your bodies as a living sacrifice, holy and pleasing to God – this is your true and proper worship. Do not conform any longer to the pattern of this world but be transformed by the renewing of your mind. Then you will be able to test and approve what God's will is – his good, pleasing and perfect will.[49]

Is there any link between what occupies your mind and self-control? Daniel Kahneman thinks there is. He explains that people tend to yield to temptation more often when they are simultaneously challenged through intensive thought processes.[50] Could this be why executives end up sleeping with their secretaries and IT workers become addicted to gambling, or vice-versa?

Pivotal in shaping this imagination is a life of rhythmic prayer and scripture reflection. Right at the heart of shaping your imagination is the Eucharist, the Lord's Table or the Breaking of Bread. Regularly revisiting the story of God through the act of corporate communion puts your vertebrae back into alignment with the rest of your spiritual spine. Your imagination is reshaped again by hearing of the love of the Father, expressed through the death and resurrection of the Son. This is brought to us through the life of the Holy Spirit and everything starts to recover its proper shape.

There is nothing more important in decision-making than the form of your imagination.

Senses

Our bodies matter in decision-making. I was speaking at a meeting in America and after it was over a small man walked up to me. I looked down on his up-raised face as we stood a short distance apart. He told me he was a Senator in the government of the USA. We talked a while and then he said, 'If I had been as tall as you I would have become President of the United States.' I think he meant it – even though I laughed – and he may have been right. I know my body matters. Every time I fly and try to fit my long body into the middle seat of an aeroplane, I know it matters. My knees poke into everything and my head sticks up above all the other heads. My bald shining head protrudes above all the other heads around almost requesting to be noticed. My body has occasionally brought me trouble. At school, my height did its work and I was the one noticed and therefore in trouble, while the little guys ran off into the playground gagging with laughter.

Our bodies matter in how we make decisions because we pick everything up through our senses. As Eugene Peterson says,

> These bodies of ours with their five senses are not impediments to the life of faith; our sensuality is not a barrier to spirituality but our only access to it... Our senses require healing and rehabilitation so that they are adequate for receiving and responding to the visitations of God's Holy Spirit.[51]

We interpret everything through our bodies. We feel, hear, see, smell and taste a sensation and then make a decision in response to it.

When you read the stories of Abraham, Sarah, Moses, Mary, Peter and Paul you see that their bodies were central to how they heard the voice of God. Seeing visions, having babies, hearing voices, walking out of prisons and vocalising their worship was the nature of their lives. The Kingdom of God will come through our bodies as we offer them up in service to God. But we will also hear God through our bodies.

What are you hearing through your body? One of the benefits of surviving a heart attack is that I have learned to listen more to my body. What is that twinge in the chest? Why that pain in my gut? Why do I want to get up and walk away from that meeting? Why does my body want to give the other body across the room a hug?

Desires

What we yearn for and crave will shape the decisions we make. Many of our decisions are shaped by what we do not have. These are often unknown and unspoken desires sedimented deep down in our hearts. We have a void in our lives even though we cannot explain what it is and where it came from. We try and address this void through an elaborate array of activities that we hope will address it. Buying more and more stuff, seeking to be famous, reading romantic fantasy novels, pornography, the adoration of money and dominating other people are just some of the ways we seek to cure our inner cravings. The truth is we are homesick for God and don't know it.

Our choices come out of our desires. The desire for food, sex, safety, companionship, excitement, honour and a meaningful life all shape the decisions I will make. These desires will be much more powerful than logic, rationality or making lists of pros and cons when making a decision. Our desires are shaping our choices long before we even know there is a choice to make.

Early in our marriage Sheila noticed how this worked with me. We would walk around a shop and I would notice a television and start to point out its good points. At first she thought I was just pointing out its good points and that is what I thought I was doing. But she noticed after a while that this was just the beginning of the process towards purchase of whatever I was notic-ing. The desire for the television was in me quite a while before I realised I was planning to buy it.

Theologian Philip Sheldrake tells us we need to befriend our desires. His point is that if we do not befriend them we will not know what they are. He says, 'Unless we feel free to own our desires in the first place we will never learn how to recognise those that are fruitful and healthy.'[52] This is very different from the idea that I should run from and deny any form of desire if I want to live a holy life. But if we are going to know ourselves, facing our desires is important. As Sheldrake says, our 'desires are best understood as our most honest experiences of ourselves.'[53] If we are going to make good decisions it will be because we run towards our desires and not away from them because, 'we act from the heart being attuned to the truth of our desires.'[54] This is true even though we may not know it.

Sheldrake also points out that if we know what our deepest desires are, and those desires are allowed to combine with God's deepest desire for us then we are in the most creative, fruitful space. If we let God's desires for us saturate through our desires we enter into a space where anything may emerge. Synergy between God and us takes place. It is like putting two chemicals together and creating a new substance, or combining red and blue and making purple. In this space there is no need to think small. Desire big things and the biggest thing God can give you is the kingdom, explains Sheldrake.

What is our deepest desire? God. We may not know it but all of our thrashing around through self-love, money-hunger, power games and sexual conquest is a broken expression of the deepest desire of all the desire for God. Why? Because we are made in God's image and it is with Him where we find our true home. We are homing pigeons that, when released, head for home. Some resist the instinct and head off in another direction, but it is in God that we are truly free and can be fully ourselves. As Charles Wesley wrote;

> Jesus confirm my heart's desire
> To work, and think and speak for thee
> Still let me guard the holy fire
> And still stir up thy gift in me.[55]

The church has been singing this verse for years as we hear the call of God inviting us to run towards our true desire which is Him. Resist this call and your decision-making will lead to eventual death. Submit to this call and enter the fullest life possible. To make a good decision we need to pray our desires, letting the Spirit of

God into each of them. Sometimes we learn we have to walk away from some of them; at other times we learn to hold on to them. Critical is that we notice them and allow God to address us regarding the desires of our hearts.

Movement Three:
Emerging from Us

We are in some manner our own parents...
giving birth to ourselves by our own free choice in
accordance with whatever we wish to be.
Gregory of Nyssa, *The Life of Moses*

Our lives are like a chick breaking through a shell or a butterfly stretching and struggling out of its cocoon, yet for mammals there is one significant difference: mammals are in slow constant growth, and become something else with each passing day. We are changing all the time. What has been delivered to us, and is working away in us, creates our future life. However, our response to these major themes of life is critical. Our culture, community, story, frameworks, identity, temperament, intuition, habits, sin, imagination, senses and desires mix together, making us the people we are. This leaves us with three other issues that propel us towards our future captivation, motivation and decisions. These three emerge out of what has come to us, and is present in us, and they set the direction for our future.

Captivation

What are you paying attention to? What are you being drawn to? What prison are you willing to be in? To whom, or what, do you say, 'I am yours'?

There are certain things that do not matter to me. When people start talking about them, I sit in silence, or try and ask questions to see if I can understand why this is important to them. I really don't care that much about cars, horse-racing, IT, maths or the occasional spelling mistake. I glaze over in conversation when these subjects surface. However, I do care about keeping my body healthy, the drama of football, the music I listen to, eating well, my family, the state of the world, God's coming kingdom, particular people's stories, my wife, theology, my house, leadership, spirituality, London and healthy organisations, amongst many other things. As you may have guessed, I care about people making good decisions. I do believe that, as Irenaeus taught us, 'the glory of God is a human being fully alive'.

All of these disinterests and passions emerge from what has been delivered to, and what is present in me. These things which have captivated me become the basis of my motivation. This sets up more important questions, for out of the captivations of your heart come your motives.

Motivation

What do I want from my life? Where do I want my life to go? What do I want to be? What do I want to feel? What do I want to avoid? If captivation is to do with what has captured my head and heart, motivation is to do with the reason why I should move in one direction or another. So it is worth asking some questions. It may take a while to go through these questions and you will need to revisit them from time to time. It is not necessary to ask them for every decision, but some may help with some decisions. Some of these questions need to be asked with a friend or two, giving you some helpful but different responses.

God Questions
– Where does my life fit in with what God is doing in the world today?
– What is God doing through this period in history?
– How has God gifted me?
– What decisions can I make that will bring God more glory?

Self Questions
– Who am I anyway?
– What is my story?
– What brings me life?
– What takes life from me?
– Am I free enough to choose suffering?

Enemy Questions
– What is the enemy doing?
– Where am I being seduced?
– What is the shape and nature of my blinkers?
– Where am I asleep?

Community Questions
– What do those who love me say about my life?
– Who do I listen to and why?
– Who do I ignore and why?
– Where is my local church going and how can I participate in it?

World Questions
- Where does the wider community need help?
- How can I help the poor; the prisoner; the blind and the oppressed?
- How can I be part of bringing in the kingdom of God in my city and beyond?

If all you are asking for is to be happy, listen to Stanley Hauerwas again:

> We rightly seek neither happiness nor pleasure in themselves; such entities are elusive. Rather we learn happiness and pleasure when we find in a faithful narrative an on-going and worthy task that sustains our lives.[56]

In my words, seek happiness itself and you are doomed to miss it. Life and happiness come out of living with and for God. You will be nourished if you do this because happiness is a by-product of something else and does not emerge if you seek it for itself.

Decisions

Decisions can go wrong. In July 1997, it was estimated that the construction of the Scottish Parliament building in Edinburgh would cost £40 million. By June 1999, the budget had shot up to £109 million. In April 2000, the parliament imposed a £195 million cap on costs. By November 2001, legislators demanded an estimate of 'final costs,' which was set at £241 million. That estimate escalated in 2002, ending the year at £294.6 million. It leaped three times more in 2003, reaching

£375.8 million in June. The building was finally completed in 2004, at an ultimate cost of approximately £431 million. Whatever went wrong in the process of this building it is clear that original intentions ended in unexpectedly expensive solutions.

Gary Klein suggests *The Premortem* to prevent such a disaster.[57] His idea is that just before you make a decision, you should go through this simple exercise of imagining that we are a year into the future. We have implemented the plan as it now exists. The outcome was a disaster. He suggests taking 5 to 10 minutes to articulate why it was a disaster in order to help identify and avoid problems before they arise.

Yet, the primary point is not the decision itself but how we make it. Daniel Kahneman warns that we make better decisions when we assume our critics are wise and just, and when we expect our decisions to be judged on how they were made rather than their outcome.[58] Michael A. Roberto would agree. With regard to leaders he explains that leaders tend to focus on the correct solutions rather than the processes that produced that solution.[59]

The key to decision-making is the process of making it rather than the decision itself. In the end if we live with open and free lives before God, our hearts tell us what to do. It may not work out as we planned, but the decision will be good and open us up for the journey of the rest of our lives walking along *Wisdom Road*.

Part Two questions

Tell the story of a really good decision you made and explain why it was good.

What prejudices do you have that influence your decision-making?

How does your life history shape your present decision-making?

What habits do you have that help you make a wise decision? What habits do you have that lead you towards a poor decision?

What part do your senses play in the decisions you make?

Why is your sense of identity so important in decision-making?

Can you trust your intuition in decision-making? If not, why not?

What are some of your culture's major characteristics? What influence do you think they play on your decision-making?

Can you own all of your desires and bring them before God in prayer? If not what would help you do this?

What do you do if you make a poor decision?

Are there any decisions you have made that need to be revisited so you can celebrate them or repent of them? What were those decisions?

What fills your imagination most of the time? What effect does that have on your decision-making?

PART THREE

Transition

After considerable thought, prayer, conversation, excitement and anxiety my wife and I decided to leave the south London church we were leading and head towards Pakistan. We were seeking to live with 'one foot raised'. The spark which ignited the idea in the first place was a rejection by other leaders of a particular initiative which I thought essential and they did not. Anyway, all things considered it was time to go. Our last Sunday in the church was memorable. We said farewell at three meetings and one of them was the Sunday School. With 120 children and many teachers present we were called out to be prayed for. As people were praying one of the teachers started to cry, and within a few seconds tears began to roll down my face. Before long many of the children were crying. Questions flooded into my head. Was I betraying these children? How could I leave and make children cry? What sort of Pastor was I to so upset children? To me this was a demonstration of how these people and crying children were going to miss me. At the end of Sunday School my wife and I took two sisters home in our car. The sisters were about seven years old. As they got into the back seat they started to cry some more. Before we pulled away and with my guilt increasing, I turned around and asked them if they were going to be alright. Quietly they said yes. Then through her tears one of them shattered my image of what was going on when she blurted out, 'Pastor...my rabbit's dead,' and through more tears her sister said, 'Now we can get a dog,' and more tears rolled down their faces. A little stunned I turned back and looked through the front windscreen. I thought they were crying about my departure and the chasm that was going to open up in their lives once I had moved on. It was not so. They had felt the emotion in the Sunday School and filled it with their own meaning. Sadly, it was not about me but about rabbits, dogs and whatever else was popping into children's minds when they saw grown people blubbering in public.

This can be the nature of transitions. You often don't know what is going on in yourself or others. Working out what God is doing can be even more difficult. It is also problematic to read the events and changing landscapes of our lives while seeking to work out what they mean. This is that which makes transitions so tricky.

To what do we need to pay attention as we go through these times of transition? I want to explain two critical Biblical themes, engage two essential scripture passages and draw two pivotal realities that should help bring perspective as we transition down *Wisdom Road*.

Live the story

As explained previously, every life is a story. How fruitful that life becomes connects to how well the person's story relates to the story of God. Scripture marks out that story moving us from Genesis to Revelation or from Creation to a new heaven and earth. Creation, fall, Israel, incarnation, redemption, ascension, Church and future hope outlines the overwhelming and mighty themes of scripture. The more we are rooted in each part of that Biblical story the more fully alive we will be and the more glory God will have. Irenaeus taught us this. For in the end the only thing that matters is The Trinity and The Kingdom of God. The story of Father, Son and Holy Spirit and what God is doing in the world through establishing the kingdom is told in the story of scripture. If we neglect parts of that huge narrative and become selective in the areas we think are preferable a price will have to be paid sooner or later. In other words, if we do not take scripture seriously we will be bamboozled, particularly in times of transition.

Let me illustrate. If you neglect the story of the Fall and therefore miss the nature of your own sinful rebellious heart, it becomes very difficult to access reality. Accessing reality is critical in decision-making. If the story of the Fall is neglected or underplayed you can easily misread yourself. Having done that, it is then much more difficult to discern what is happening around you. Skimming over the story of the Fall will lead you to becoming the victim of your own eccentric biases because you will not have been able to track the true nature of your own heart. It is the Holy Spirit who gives us awareness of our broken lives in a broken world, granting us the humility to enter into glorious acts of refreshing repentance. When we repent and submit ourselves to God and what He is doing in the world our judgement and discernment return, or at least have the chance to.

On the other hand, if you miss the future hope ahead and fail to anticipate it, another price is to be paid. The world becomes small and you fail to make decisions in the light of the huge future intentions of God. It is only in the light of an anticipation of a new heaven and new earth that we can come to an understanding of what has happened in our lives and what is happening as we pass through times of transition. We stumble when we do not have this future hope setting our hearts on fire when envisaging our future. Another cost of underplaying this part of the story is loss of patience. If you are living without a rich anticipation of the future of God it is much more difficult to delay the gratifications of success which life often offers. Misread the future and you misunderstand the present.

To flourish through times of transition we need to live the story of God and not the particular parts of the story we prefer. All the lenses of the story need to be lined up adequately so we can see as clearly as possible the place where we find ourselves, the transition we are in and what could be the way forward in the future.

Permanent transition

Walter Brueggemann explains how the Psalms work and in doing so explains how life works. He puts everything in a context of transition, identifying three movements through which we all travel.[60] He divides the Psalms up into three; Psalms of orientation, Psalms of disorientation and Psalms of new orientation. David G. Firth picks up on this and renames these divisions as Psalms of the ordered world, the disordered world and reordered world.[61] All the Psalms are intended to be prayed as we go through these various stages. 'Ordered' is when life is where we want it to be. 'Disordered' usually describes what happens soon after we think it is ordered. 'Reordered' is when through God's work and word a fresh position is established and we feel ordered again. The idea is permanent transition both in our conversation with God and in how we engage with life in the everyday.

This is how life works. We think all is under control and we are doing well. Then some wave hits us and the ship begins to roll, challenging the course we have set. As Captain we take corrective measures and equilibrium is established until another wave hits or the weather system changes bringing a new set of issues and decisions. This is the way it will be because we are forever engaging particular persons, fresh conditions and our own complex lives as we seek to move forward. We are on a continual journey through order, disorder and reorder even if we never move home or church. The only issue is the intensity of the shifting sea and the particular weather system we are living through at the time.[62]

Realising that we are in a place of permanent change is critical in doing well through transitions. Perhaps the illusion is to imagine that we are ever in a safe place of orientation, order and stability where nothing alters, when in fact the world is swirling around us all of the time and we are in continual change. Ralph D. Stacey feels that traveling towards equilibrium is no way forward; winning requires a journey away from equilibrium.[63] Perhaps he has read the Psalms. The truth is that everything is in transition all of the time, be it at a glacial crawl or tsunami thunder. It is going to be challenging to adapt to transitions and change unless we work with these categories of order, disorder and reorder in one form or another throughout the whole of our lives. The Psalms are key texts for transition because they are the praises, prayers and complaints of the people who have gone through it before us.

Jesus at Nazareth

Transition was intended in Nazareth. The shifting relationship between the leader and the led – or in Nazareth's case the not-to-be-led – is starkly explained in Mark 6:1-6. This is how I see the story: Jesus arrived with is disciples in Nazareth, His home town. Before long the relational distance between Jesus and the people of Nazareth became apparent. Things had clearly changed. This was not only home town for Jesus it was also 'small town' because Nazareth would not face the big world Jesus was opening before their eyes. It seemed that the people of Nazareth could not adjust to what they saw in front of them. Jesus was the boy to them but now he was returning as the man or, even worse, a leader. It appears His transformation had outstripped their ability to adapt to what He now was. Jesus even had a following of disciples and assistants. Home town Nazareth appeared to struggle with this. You can hear the relational gears grinding and jamming together as

Nazareth tried to work out what was in front of them and who this Jesus was now.

Nazareth failed to navigate the transition in a healthy way. They preferred their unbelief and denial. It seems like it was all too much for them to grasp. Many were amazed at Jesus' teaching but others – or the same people – took offence at Him. It is as though they were paralysed in the middle of the road as the twin head-lights of His wisdom and miracles bore down on them. They asked the questions, 'Isn't this the carpenter? Isn't this Mary's son and the brother of James, Joseph, Judas and Simon? Aren't His sisters here with us?'[64] It could also be that they just decided to be offended, therefore giving themselves a way out of dealing with the stunning realities of what was happening through Jesus. If He was what His life demonstrated then the people of Nazareth had deep challenges to face and new thoughts to think. The implications were immense.

How did they resolve this internal conflict? Who can know the exact motivations of the people of Nazareth? Yet boxing Jesus up seemed to be the solution. It appears that they needed to put Jesus into a box so they could manage Him. They were not aware that the box was ridiculously small and was destined to be shattered by the resurrection. We have in Nazareth a commu-nity that could not cope with the transition of a boy becoming a man and a follower becoming a leader. The people of Nazareth had congealed into their final selves and little could be done. Nazareth refused to be men-tored by the one they nurtured. It seems that they could not cope with a prophet who to them was a little boy. Their inability to change amazed Jesus and rather than it being described as an adjustment problem or some other minor weakness, He described it in much more challenging language as a 'lack of faith'.[65]

Peter and Cornelius

In contrast to the people of Nazareth are Peter and Cornelius. Their story of transition is explained in Acts 10. Cornelius was a centurion in the Italian Regiment. He was devout, God-fearing and generous. He lived in Caesarea, the Roman capital over Judea. He would have been leading up to 600 men in his Roman cohort, who were probably archers. Cornelius would have worked his way up through the ranks being a non-commissioned officer.[66] He was helpful to the poor and had healthy prayer habits. Yet he was a non-Jew leading an army of occupation. He may well have been sympathetic to Judaism, but he was not a follower of Christ until a meeting happened in his house. Cornelius prayed at three o'clock in the afternoon and had a vision of an angel. The messenger spoke Cornelius' name and filled him with fear while telling him to go and get Simon Peter. Cornelius sent three of his men to complete the task.

Transitions do not come with much greater intensity than the one God offered Peter through his roof-top vision. We know Peter well. He was the courageous walk-on-water Apostle. He was a devout Jew and now a leader in the emerging church. God had used him wonderfully, particularly after the resurrection and the outpouring of the Holy Spirit. He was in the beautiful place of Joppa, which is now Jaffa, part of coastal Tel Aviv. He went up onto his roof to pray. In prayer he had a trance and a vision was given to him. For a Jew this would have been a horrific vision. On a sheet lowered down from heaven came four-footed animals, reptiles and birds. Then a voice said, 'Get up Peter, kill and eat'. He replied, 'Surely not Lord!' Peter received this vision three times. This was not the first time Peter had had to hear something three times.

While Peter was hesitating, doing his 'wondering' and 'thinking' he found that God had provided some leverage that gave Peter momentum. A Roman soldier and his servants were outside his house just as the Spirit had said. Peter was now in significant transition. His visionary trance was changing into concrete reality. This experience was now very real and standing in front of him in the shape of three men calling out his name. The centurion's messengers wanted Peter to come and speak to them at Cornelius' house in Caesarea. Peter's world was being inverted and transformed yet he responded positively to this request.

Peter went through his normal prayer routine and his world was shattered in this place of prayer. He was a Jew and was restricted in what he could eat.[67] In his vision were clean and unclean animals and it scandalised him. Yet, this was also a staggering vision of future Jew and Gentile relationships to be expressed in the future church. Peter was being introduced to the unthinkable because of the new thing God was doing through Cornelius. This was not only Peter receiving fresh vision, it was a picture of the future shape of the worldwide church. Peter said, 'it is against our law for a Jew to associate with or visit a Gentile'[68] but that is precisely what he was doing. Up to this point the Apostle was a religious sectarian but now he had the radical challenges of spectacular transition pressing against his nose. God had just shown him that no race is better than another. Nothing was ever going to be the same again for Peter or for the church.

Cornelius and Peter were on a journey towards each other, a journey that Peter would find very difficult. But it was Peter's ability to be shaped by Cornelius that helped change him, and in the end changed the world. If Peter had not made that transition the gospel could have been locked up for years in some sectarian scheme and might never have broken out into the Gentile world.

What can we take from these two themes and passages when it comes to walking down *Wisdom Road*? What should shape our imaginations from these themes and passages? I want to focus on two areas.

Live out of control

I have always enjoyed my times of transition. They have always been fresh places of thought and release but this is not so for many. Each of us has to find the grace, imagination, revelation and practice to find our own way through.

One of the reasons why transitions can be so challenging is because we feel vulnerable and out of control for as long as they last. The time of transition is the time of disconnection where everything is being shifted from one place to another. This theme of living out of control is summed up by the ever-quotable Stanley Hauerwas, who writes:

Learning to live out of control, learning to live without trying to force contingency into conformity because of our desperate need for security, I take as a resource for discovering alternatives that would otherwise not be present.[69]

Think about that for a while. Eugene H. Peterson expresses much the same thing.[70] If we are able to let go of the controls of our lives, who knows what blessings may come our way that we would not otherwise have noticed if we had kept control? We cannot live as if we are the sole producers of our own lives. Rather, living out of control, yet rooted in the middle of the story of God, opens up our imaginations to all the possibilities offered in times of transition. We cannot control the various events and seasons which come to us as we move through order, disorder and reorder. What we can control is our response to them.

Peter was able to live out of control but the people of Nazareth were not. It was as Peter responded to his vision that revelation happened. Significant breakthrough took place in his imagination and world view as he responded to the vision when he merged back into the material reality of Joppa after his trance. Peter explained later that, through his vision, inaccurate and inappropriate judgements were challenged: 'God has shown me that I should not call anyone impure or unclean' (10:28), and his parochial local world became global: 'God does not show favouritism but accepts those from every nation who fear him and do right' (10:35). This only came to him as he was willing to go with the startling vision of what God was calling him to do and live out of control. It is remarkable how many of us can be so controlling when the process of transition takes place. My guess is that fear quietly injects itself into our hearts and solidifies in our heads so we can't think straight. To flourish through transition we need to learn to let go. Peter could do this. Nazareth could not.

Mentored life

We are all being shaped and mentored in one way or another. All of our assumptions around how life works and our understanding of common sense demonstrate the influence of culture, family and relationships. We are being formed through our choices and what they come to mean for us. Right at the heart of this formation is the company we have kept and now keep. 'Do not be deceived,' says Paul, 'God cannot be mocked. People reap what they sow'.[71] Our ability to cope with times of transition will be related to the company we have kept before the transition takes place. Who have been the people who have shaped our hearts and minds?

Right at the core of transition and living on *Wisdom Road* is mentoring. What ideas have mentored me? What desires mentor me? Who is mentoring me through this transition process? Who am I mentoring? Where am I rooted in my head and heart as the transition takes place? We cannot know ourselves alone. Without community to teach us who we are we are lost in a desert of introspection and guesswork. Walking through transition with others is vital to doing it well. I want to identify three areas of mentoring which will help as we navigate transition.

MENTORED BY GOD

Jim Houston clarifies what a Christian is in explaining that becoming a Christian is a destruction of one's identity built around the ruins of self-enclosure.[72] Becoming a Christian is to do with the shift from just being self-defined, self-focused and individual to becoming a 'person' who becomes who they are because of their communion with God and their community with other people.

Understanding ourselves as a 'person' in this sense is central to transitioning well. This is at the core of what God is doing in our lives and is our deepest need. Kierkegaard taught us that human being's highest achievement is to let God be able to help him [or her]. In one sentence he resets the cultural clock of the western world and explains to us what human success looks like. Success is being mentored by God in relationship with Father, Son and Holy Spirit.

Therefore, right at the heart of transitions are the practices and disciplines of the faith and in particular prayer. Scripture is also central to the process. Reading scripture not only for information but for formation shapes the way in which we respond to God, the world and ourselves. A prayerful contemplative engagement with scripture nourishes us on the journey during times of transition. It was in the place of prayer that Peter was mentored by God through receiving his vision and a whole new world opened up for him. His ordered world became disordered but was reordered as he listened to God.

If God does not mentor us through scripture and prayer then we will be mentored by other things which will shape our heads and hearts. Money, sex, power, fear, time and place will tend to dominate and enslave our decision-making processes during times of change. Being mentored through scripture and in prayer by Father, Son and Holy Spirit will keep us nourished and receptive in times of transition and able to spot the serpent's tail.

MENTORED BY COMMUNITY

Mentoring is usually seen as a dialogue between two people. The idea is that someone who is a bit further along the road helps someone just beginning the journey. We have many examples of this in scripture with Elijah and Elisha, Naomi and Ruth, Barnabas and Paul, Paul and almost everyone else in the New Testament. But the weight of the mentoring process needs to be communal rather than one-on-one relationships, important as they are.

Jesus developed His disciples in community. He called the group into existence and formed it around himself as the teacher. The motivation behind His mentoring was not to discover the potential of each disciple so they could live their lives well or that they may have a sense of fulfilment. They were called together so they could establish the church. Jesus called, taught, walked with and released His disciples so they would become the leaders of the emerging church. This communal mentoring theme continued into the first centuries of the church.[73] However, keeping good company in communal mentoring is important. If you were mentored by the Nazareth community it would have been a toxic experience. Keeping the right company is critical when it comes to shaping our imaginations and the decisions we make. However, keeping the right company does not mean keeping safe company.

I have been the member of several mentoring groups. Some have been built around a leader and some have been more peer-focused. The relationships built up in these groups often survive after the conclusion of the group. Many of these sorts of groups go on for decades. These relationships are vital at times of transition. They often contain people who love you but are not so interested in what you can do for them or the particular contribution you can make to their lives. They usually contain people who are more interested in you as a person rather than in what you can deliver. This is what makes them valuable, particularly in times of transition. They are particularly helpful in absorbing the shock of change and in working out the possible options for the future.

MENTORED BY A PERSON

If you are blessed you may also have a person who is your mentor, this is a person who 'with God-given capacity and God-given responsibility to influence a specific group of God's people towards His purposes for the group,'[74] mentors you. Skilled mentors are able to notice our story and see how it connects or disconnects with the story of God. They are able to challenge us and call us out of our self-indulgence and fantasies so we may re-engage with God's story. They are often able to notice where we are in terms of order, disorder and reorder, sometimes pointing out that what we considered to be disorder is actually reordering or what we considered as order needs some disordering. They can become Cornelius-like figures in our lives, obediently responding to God's initiative and preventing us from developing Nazareth-like stubbornness when called by God to change. Good mentors lead us out of our boxed-up lives and point out the horizons and possibilities ahead. In doing so they prepare us for the next phase of ministry and pastoral responsibility, when we will do the same thing for others who are negotiating their way through the labyrinth of money, sex, power, time and place.

Living the story of God, allowing room for our reordering, disavowing the unbelief of Nazareth and being open to the voice of God, is cultivated in us as we learn to live out of control and experience a mentored life. At least this is what I have learned on the journey so far. What is the one virtue that brings this together? Courage. We will need the courage to say no to a little life and yes to the biggest life we can possibly live. We will need courage to get back on *Wisdom Road* if we have wandered off it. All this is preparation for the time when a weeping little girl bursts your vain imaginings by telling you, 'Pastor... my rabbit's dead,' and introduces you to the realities of transition on *Wisdom Road*.

Our lives become smaller if we try to live safely and do not focus on how we will flourish. If we focus on safety we may miss out on the wonder of a brilliantly lived life. Like horses in a race we may not even see the possibilities because of the safety blinkers attached to the side of our heads. The insightful Frederick Buechner explained that God's will for us is usually found where the world's greatest need and our deepest desire meet. Where is the intersection between these two realities? This may be the zone where we learn to live our lives well. Ignatius of Loyola described the ideal Jesuit as 'living with one foot raised,' so always ready to respond to emerging opportunities. If both feet are stuck to the ground, do you have the freedom to move when God says it is time to dance? Finally, and overwhelmingly, how does God get the most glory out of your life? Given that we are not the point of our own lives and that God is the point, how does your life bring most glory to Him?

Then, with one foot raised, we make a decision – bold, informed, wise and free – as we put our next foot to the ground and head down *Wisdom Road*.

Part Three questions

Why do some people find transition fearful? Why are others not scared of it at all?

Who and what is mentoring you as you walk down *Wisdom Road*?

Is it a helpful thing to learn to 'live out of control'? In what ways is it helpful?

If we are living in a world of permanent transition, what do we need to learn to survive and flourish through these transitions?

Why is it important to walk with God through scripture as you walk down *Wisdom Road*?

Are there particular books or stories in scripture that help you through transition?

What do you want to be like twenty years from now? Who do you want to be like twenty years from now?

References

1. Walter Isaacson, 2011, *Steve Jobs*, New York: Simon & Schuster, p. 453.

2. Daily Prayers of the Church of England https://churchofengland.org/prayer-worship/join-us-in-daily-prayer.aspx

3. Matthew 10:16 New International Version (NIV). Unless otherwise stated, all Scripture references are from the NIV.

4. 1 Kings 3:9

5. Phil 1:9-11

6. Psalm 1:3

7. James 3:17-18

8. E. Randolph Richards and Brandon J. O'Brien, 2012, *Misreading Scripture with Western Eyes*, Downers Grove IL: IVP.

9. Matthew 7:24-27

10. Miroslav Volf, 2005, *Free of Charge,* Zondervan, p.33.

11. John 1:14

12. Luke 15:20-24

13. James K.A. Smith, 2009, *Desiring the Kingdom: Worship, Worldview and Cultural Formation*, Grand Rapids: Baker Academic.

14. Samuel Wells, 2004, *Improvisation: The Drama of Christian Ethics,* SPCK.

15. Matthew 16:25

16. Read J. Michael Sparough, Jim Manney, Tim Hipskind, 2010, *What's Your Decision: How to Make Choices with Confidence and Clarity*, Loyola Press, where they explore an Ignatian approach to decision-making.

17. Ignatian Spiritual Exercise 23.

18. Luke 1:38

19. Matthew 6:10

20. Matt 6:19-21; Luke 12:32ff

21. James L. Wakefield, 2005, *Sacred Listening: Discovering the Exercises of Ignatius Loyola*, Baker Books. Wakefield adapts the exercises of Ignatius for a Protestant audience.

22. Stephen Cottrell, 2007, *Do Nothing to Change Your Life*, London: Church House Publishing.

23. Psalm 1:2-3

24. Rowan Williams in an interview with David Hare said, 'if I'm not absolutely paralysed by the question, "Am I right? Am I safe?" then there are

more things I can ask of myself.' *The Guardian*, 'God's Boxer' interview, 8 July 2011.

25. Read John Stott, 2007, *The Living Church: Convictions of a lifelong pastor*, Inter-Varsity Press, and feel the love and absorb the clarity of Stott's reflections on the church. See especially 'I have a dream of a living church', p. 197-182.

26. *The Times*, Saturday, 3 April 2010 p. 89.

27. Michael A. Roberto, 2009 *The Critical Art of Decision Making*, DVD The Teaching Company.

28. For an initial look at the long list of possible biases look at http://en.wiki-pedia.org/wiki/List_of_cognitive_biases

29. Diane Vaughan, 1996, *The Challenger Launch Decision: Risky Technology, Culture and Deviance at NASA*, University of Chicago Press.

30. http://www.bc.edu/bc_org/rvp/pubaf/chronicle/v4/F01/VAUGHAN/VAUGHAN.html

31. Stanley Hauerwas, 2009, *The Peaceable Kingdom,* London: SCM Press, p. 17.

32. Ibid, p. 129.

33. Smith, *Desiring the Kingdom*, p. 26

34. http://www.gehlhausen.com/Files/Family/The%20Four%20Temperaments.pdf

35. These temperaments were largely based on the Greek Gods of Apollo, Dionysus, Epimetheus and Prometheus.

36. http://www.colorcode.com/myprofile/ It goes on to say, 'Yellows need to look good socially, and friendships command a high priority in their lives. Yellows are happy, articulate, engaging of others and crave adventure. Easily distracted, they can never sit still for long. They embrace each day in the 'present tense' and choose people who, like themselves, enjoy a curious nature. Yellows are charismatic, spontaneous, and positive; but can also be irresponsible, obnoxious, and forgetful. When you deal with a yellow, take a positive, upbeat approach and promote light-hearted, creative, and fun interactions'.

37. 1 Corinthians 12:14-27

38. **Sanguine.** The Sanguine temperament personality is fairly extroverted. People of a sanguine temperament tend to enjoy social gatherings, making new friends and tending to be boisterous. They are usually quite creative and often daydream. However, some alone time is crucial for those of this temperament. Sanguine can also mean very sensitive, compassionate and thoughtful. Sanguine personalities generally struggle with following tasks all the way through, are chronically late, and tend to be forgetful and sometimes a little sarcastic. Often, when pursuing a new hobby, interest is lost quickly when it ceases to be engaging or fun. They are very much

people persons. They are talkative and not shy. People of sanguine temperament can often be emotional. **Choleric.** A person who is choleric is a doer. They have a lot of ambition, energy, and passion, and try to instil it in others. They can dominate people of other temperaments, especially phlegmatic types. Many great charismatic military and political figures were choleric. They like to be leaders and in charge of everything. They can be very manipulative. **Melancholic.** A person who is a thoughtful ponderer has a melancholic disposition. Often very considerate and rather worried if they cannot be on time for events, melancholics can be highly creative in activities such as poetry and art – and can become occupied with the tragedy and cruelty in the world. A *melancholic* is also often a perfectionist. They are often self-reliant and independent; one negative part of being a melancholic is sometimes they can get so involved in what they are doing they forget to think of others. **Phlegmatic.** Phlegmatics tend to be self-content and kind. They can be very accepting and affectionate. They may be very receptive and shy and often prefer stability to uncertainty and change. They are very consistent, relaxed, calm, rational, curious and observant, making them good administrators. They can also be very passive-aggressive.

39. Daniel Kahneman, 2011, *Thinking, Fast and Slow*, London: Penguin Books, p. 67.

40. Malcolm Gladwell, 2006, *Blink*, London: Penguin Books.

41. http://www.ucg.org/christian-living/seven-types-intelligence/ The seven types are logical-mathematical, bodily-kinaesthetic, visual-spatial, interpersonal (emotional), intrapersonal, musical and verbal-linguistic

42. Jeremiah 17:9, *The Message*.

43. Romans 8:26

44. Tom Wright, 2010, *Virtue Reborn*, London: SPCK, p. 92. He is particularly referring to the Sermon on the Mount.

45. Ibid, p.90.

46. Hauerwas, *Peaceable Kingdom*, p.47.

47. Ibid, p.48.

48. Phillip Sheldrake, *Brief History of Spirituality*, London: Blackwell, p.86.

49. Romans 12:1-2

50. Kahneman, *Thinking*, p. 41.

51. Eugene Peterson, 1997, *Subversive Spirituality*, Cambridge: Wm. B. Eerdmans p. 14.

52. Sheldrake, *Spirituality*, p. 16.

53. Ibid, p. 18.

54. Ibid, p. 105.

55. Charles Wesley, 'O thou who camest from above', Public Domain.

56. Hauerwas, *Peaceable Kingdom,* p. 48.

57. See Gary Klein, 2004, *The Power of Intuition,* New York: Doubleday, p. 98–101.

58. Kahneman, *Thinking,* p. 250.

59. Roberto, *Decision Making.*

60. Walter Brueggemann, 1984, *The Message of the Psalms,* Minneapolis: Augsburg.

61. David G. Firth, 2005, *Hear, O Lord: A Spirituality of the Psalms,* Cliff College Publishing.

62. It is possible to live through all of these phases at one time depending on the various spheres of life we inhabit.

63. Ralph C. Stacey, 1993, *Strategic Management and Organisational Dynamics,* London: Pitman Publishing.

64. Mark 6:3

65. Mark 6:6

66. Richard N. Longnecker, 'Acts', in Frank E. Gaebelein ed., 1981, *The Expositor's Bible Commentary,* vol 9, p. 385.

67. See Leviticus 11.

68. Acts 10:28

69. Stanley Hauerwas, 2010, *Hannah's Child,* London: SCM Press, p. 137.

70. See Eugene H. Peterson, 2007, *The Jesus Way,* London: Hodder, p. 276, where Peterson describes Hauerwas as 'my theologian of choice as a conversation partner.'

71. Galatians 6:7

72. James H. Houston, 2002, *The Mentored Life: From Individualism to Personhood,* Colorado Springs: NavPress.

73. Edward L. Smither, 2008, *Augustine as Mentor: A Model for Preparing Spiritual Leaders,* Nashville: B&H Publishing, p.90-91. Smither also points out the importance of correspondence and Church Councils as critical mentoring tools, and notes that Cyprian, Pachomius, Basil of Caesarea, and Augustine all place an emphasis on mentoring the group and not only the individual.

74. Robert Clinton, 1988, *The Making of a Leader,* Colorado Springs: Nav Press, p. 245.